John Watson

Sketches of British Sporting Fishes

John Watson

Sketches of British Sporting Fishes

ISBN/EAN: 9783742899163

Manufactured in Europe, USA, Canada, Australia, Japa

Cover: Foto ©Thomas Meinert / pixelio.de

Manufactured and distributed by brebook publishing software
(www.brebook.com)

John Watson

Sketches of British Sporting Fishes

SKETCHES

OF

BRITISH SPORTING FISHES

BY

JOHN WATSON,

AUTHOR OF "SYLVAN FOLK," "A YEAR IN THE FIELDS," ETC., ETC.

LONDON: CHAPMAN AND HALL

LIMITED.

1890

PREFATORY NOTE.

THE contents of the following pages have no pretension to be more than the slightest possible sketches. The subject-matter has, for the most part, been gleaned directly from the waterside, and should be looked upon more as the notes of a naturalist than the jottings of an angler. The paper on Grayling was kindly contributed by a friend, who loves this plucky sporting fish as the Norman William is said to have loved the wild red deer.

J. W.

CONTENTS.

I.

PAGE

SALMON 1

II.

TROUT 13

III.

GRAYLING 21

IV.

PIKE 28

V.

PERCH 36

VI.

ROACH AND RUDD 44

VII.

CARP AND BREAM 51

VIII.

BARBEL, DACE, AND GUDGEON 63

IX.

CONCERNING SMALL FRY—I. 71

X.

CONCERNING SMALL FRY—II. 83

XI.

ONCE SILVER STREAMS 93

XII.

FISH STEWS 100

XIII.

PAGE

THE DEPOPULATION AND RESTOCKING OF TROUT-STREAMS   107

XIV.

WATER POACHERS 117

XV.

THE FISH-POACHER   123

XVI.

EPHEMERÆ 130

XVII.

A KING AMONG ANGLERS   135

BRITISH SPORTING FISHES.

SALMON.

WITH all our practical and scientific means of investigation, it is strange how much remains to be known about the salmon. There are certain phases of its life-history which are as yet a mystery, and which the closest scrutiny has not enabled us to unravel. Its food, its migrations, its spawning, its very appearance vary in different rivers, though peculiar local conditions doubtless account for much of the confusion which now exists. There is one fact in connection with the species which is placed outside the range of controversy, and which ought to prove valuable in the future. It is now definitely known that in the great majority of cases salmon return to spawn in the river where they were bred. What it is that enables a fresh-run fish to do this is not clearly known, though Buckland in his life was strongly of the opinion that the chief sense employed was that of smell. This, however, is immaterial, though it is an important fact that the salmon returns to its old haunts.

This aristocrat of the waters is essentially a sea-fish ; and at whatever season it may enter a river, the act is closely connected with the reproduction of its kind. Salmon begin to "run" in English rivers from May to December, though the autumn months mark the time of the heaviest migrations. The ascent of the rivers is not rapid. Even if these be bank-full and the usual obstructions passable, the fish do not hurry, but love to examine the ground as they go.

There is a deafening roar from the water, and the impalpable spray constitutes a constant maze of translucent vapour. Ever and anon a big fish throws its silvery form many feet above the water, endeavouring to clear the obstacle. Many times it is beaten back, but at last gains a ledge, and by a concentrated effort manages to throw itself into the still, deep water beyond. Instead of leaping, the female fish try to run through the foam, and on from stone to stone, until a last leap takes them over. In the absence of salmon-passes, many of the fish are picked from the rocks dead, and the majority of these prove to be males. This preponderance is also noticeable on the

spawning-beds, though why it should be so is
not definitely known. The "redds" are selected
where the river is clearest and purest—where
there is bright gravel and an absence of sediment. As the she-fish settles to spawning, she
scoops out a hole in the sheltering gravel, and is
closely attended by her mate. He indulges in
many beautiful evolutions, and guards her against
every enemy. When spawning is concluded, it
is found that she has nearly a thousand eggs for
every pound of her live weight. Take a handful
of these pearly pink eggs, and examine them.
Although delicate in appearance, they are not
only capable of standing great pressure, but
are so elastic, that if one be thrown down
it will rebound like an indiarubber ball. Once
the eggs are hatched, the fry afford delicate
morsels to a whole host of aquatic creatures—
birds, insects, and fishes themselves. When the
fry attain to the "smelt" stage, they have an
equally hard time of it, and the number of their
enemies is hardly to be reckoned.

Salmon are local in their haunts and habits,
and on a favourite "redd" numbers of fish are
found. This hardly conduces to success, for when
the beds are full of fish they are routed over and
over until much spawn is spoiled; and it is when
salmon are abundant and lie closely that the

dreaded disease makes its appearance. This
shows as a white fungus about the head and
shoulders, and gradually spreads until the fish
sickens and dies. Hardly anything is known
about the disease, except that it is infectious.
Newly-run salmon that come in contact with
affected fish soon develop it; and when once it
breaks out, there is scarcely an individual but
what shows signs of the fungus. Spates and
floods tend to eradicate it, and these alone.

An interesting fact anent salmon is that they
produce hybrids with other fish. They breed
freely with brown-trout, brook-trout, also those
peculiar to Loch Leven; and this is the more
remarkable as the offspring from this cross
in no wise sacrifice their fertility. That salmon
and trout are commonly found on the same
"redd" has long been known to poachers, though
scientists have only admitted the fact recently.
Here is an actual incident. Upon one occasion
a poacher found a freshly-run male salmon watching over a female, the former of which he gaffed.
Knowing that a second suitor would soon take
the place of the first, he allowed the she-fish to
remain. A second male attended her, a third,
and a fourth, she starting down-stream each time
her lord was taken. Upon her fifth return she
brought back a large yellow trout, and so much

interest did the proceeding excite, that for a time the two were left unmolested. The spawn was then taken, hatched on a grill, and large, healthy fry was the result.

Here the normal life-history of the salmon must be recurred to. After a brief period spent upon the spawning-beds, the breeding-fish return to salt water. At this time they are in a wretchedly poor condition—lean and lank, the flesh loose and "flabby." The spawned fish are known as "kelts." Once, however, in the food-abounding sea, they quickly recover condition, feeding now, for the most part, on shrimps. And here, for a time, we may leave them, whilst we return to the river. The eggs are hatched, the fry have absorbed their yolk-sacs, and the tiny things are scattered over the higher river reaches. As the warm days develop the soft-winged ephemeræ, the fry begin to forage for themselves, and soon comes a crisis in their life-history. Some day a brown spate comes from the hills, the water is turgid, and in shoals the silvery samlets rush down to the sea to explore its wide world of waters. They usually travel with the first floods of April and May, and having by this time assumed the migratory dress, are termed "smolts." At one time it was supposed that the young of salmon left their

river-nursery for the sea during the first spring,
but this is not so. Some few early-spawned
fish may do this, but the majority wait until
the following year. Once in the sea, smolts
grow at a rapid rate, and after from four to
twelve months, return to the rivers where they
were bred, as " grilse." As the grilse make up-
stream they are pretty, silvery fish, and afford
good sport. They vary greatly in weight, and
it is somewhat curious that, upon their first
arrival, they are invariably covered with " sea-
lice." These uninvited guests are soon ridded
in the rivers, as they do not long survive im-
mersion in fresh water.

Entering rivers to spawn, going down to the
sea, and re-entering the rivers, constitutes, shortly,
the life-history of the salmon. Speaking generally,
it feeds but little in fresh water, and loses weight;
in the sea it feeds ravenously, and increases at
a most remarkable rate. One British-killed
salmon has attained to seventy pounds in weight
and four-and-a-half feet in length. This fish was
taken in the Tay, and a cast of it is now in
the Buckland Museum. Although this was a
monster fish, almost without precedent, yet forty-
pound salmon are not at all uncommon. In
rivers the food of the salmon consists mainly
of ephemeræ and their larvæ, worms, and the

spawn and fry of various fresh-water fishes. In the sea its food is more varied and abundant. Salmon are invariably found in the proximity of shrimp - grounds, and they devour enormous quantities of sand-eels. That, however, upon which they most depend for sustenance is the myriad fry of the coarser sea-fish. Of course, it is difficult to follow the fish in its migrations in salt water; but, from several sources, hints may be had of its wanderings. Salmon seem to swim in the sea in comparatively small droves, probably of from twenty to a hundred; and it is certain that they are much given to hugging the coast-line. They stay long on banks or in channels, where favourite food is to be had, and are only driven off by receding tides. In spring and summer they do not inhabit deep water, but keep more to the banks, usually in only a few fathoms of water. At this time the sand-launce is much fed upon, as is the sea-urchin in its earlier stages. Mr. Huxley asserts—and his assertion stands almost alone — that the salmon's food chiefly consists of a numerous class of small creatures (entomostracous crustacea) found in semi-solid masses upon the surface of deep water; in short, that the salmon swims in a species of animal soup, in which it has merely to open its mouth and swallow what enters it.

Every creature here named as constituting the food of salmon has been found in the fish itself, though, as these soft-bodied creatures are so quickly digested, positive identification is rendered most difficult. Both salmon and trout have the power (which, under certain circumstances, they exercise) of ejecting any food recently taken when they find themselves hooked or in the meshes of a net. Quantities of herrings have been found thus ejected. That the salmon is a voracious feeder in the sea is certain, and whilst in its native element it lays up a large store of fat—a fact which probably accounts for its feeding but little in rivers. Like many other sea creatures, it is able to draw upon this provision during its periods of semi-fasting, as when on the spawning-beds. The intestines of sea-salmon are frequently almost buried in layers of fat, and another coating lies between the skin and the flesh. Salmon constantly confined in fresh water, as in lochs, and those which can take the sea at pleasure, are altogether different fishes. The flesh of the latter is firm and pink, that of the former white and insipid. As salmon grow rapidly, they probably do not attain. to a great age.

After the salmon and trout proper come a number of close cousins, concerning which much

confusion still exists. This, however, is not for
want of attention to the subject by naturalists.
The discrimination between species and varieties
is often a difficult matter, and in this connection,
no rule which has been laid down has held good
for any length of time. This is owing to the
fact that fresh-water fishes adapt themselves to
local circumstances more effectually and more
rapidly than any other class of creatures. In
fact, in the family under notice, it is hardly
known what are salmon and what are trout;
and the only satisfactory division is that of
migratory and non-migratory species. These
include the salmon, brown brook-trout, bull-trout,
salmon-trout, gillaroo, sewin, short-headed salmon,
great lake-trout, Loch Leven trout, a number of
others, and some char. Many of these are nothing more than varieties with local peculiarities,
probably produced by different conditions of
food and water in their particular haunts. The
inclination of naturalists has been to evolve
species from mere varieties by a process of
hair-splitting; but in the future, and as the laws
which govern evolution become better understood, the tendency will probably be the other way.

The salmon- or sea-trout, is, as its name
implies, one of the migratory species. It is
common in most salmon rivers, and is widely

distributed throughout the country. In Ireland it is the white-trout, in Cornwall and Devon the peal. Although not now so abundant as formerly, it is still taken in quantities in the salmon rivers of both our east and west coasts. Like its congeners, the salmon-trout enters rivers to spawn, leaving them again after depositing its eggs. As rivers are "early" and "late," the fish ascend from the sea through summer and autumn, spawning from October to December. The kelts descend during the spring months at the same time as the smelts, after which the latter rapidly increase in size.

The sea-trout is one of the favourite fishes of the angler. It is usually game for some weeks after trout are "out," and considerable interest attaches to its coming. The fisherman watches for signs of the sea-fish in autumn as eagerly as he hoped for the advent of the swallow in spring. The presence of the former betokens long night-fishings and abundant sport. He is not so wary as the trout, and a far more assiduous feeder. In September, anglers who love autumn fishing move down to the deeps to meet the coming army. The fish enter the river in shoals, and every freshet enables them to gain a higher reach. As soon as they have had time to disperse, the angler takes the self-same stand from which only the

frost drove him last year, and once more he tries
all his old flies. The sea-trout are not slow
to take his lures, and many a stout fight is made
in the darkness. More often than not, the fisher
knows every hole of the pool, and fight as it
may, the game fish cannot shake him off. He
mechanically leads the fish in the darkness, and
can hardly discern it, even as he takes it off
the hook. At the coming of day, his creel is full
of beautiful fish, every one of which has tried
his skill, but has eventually come to his basket.
If the fish have run early, this fine sport sometimes lasts for a couple of months, and for the
salmon or trout-fisher it finishes the season.

It requires a practical fisherman to at once
detect the sea-trout. Speaking generally, it
resembles its cousin the brown brook-trout, except
that one is done in bluish-silver, the other in
brown and gold. The water in which it happens
to be for the time being, has much influence
upon its colour, and the silvery sea-fish becomes
more like the trout in proportion as it stays in
fresh water. The white-trout, which run in
autumn, range from half-a-pound, to three, four,
and five pounds in weight; fish exceeding this
being uncommon. The food of this species
varies considerably, according to haunt and
season. In the sea it is an omnivorous feeder,

and is particularly fond of small crustaceæ, sand-hoppers, and other marine creatures. As it approaches the estuaries of rivers, its food becomes more general, and when it enters them, the winged water-flies constitute almost its sole diet.

Another member of the *Salmonidæ* is the bull-trout, said to be a species by some, by others only a variety. It is found in many rivers common to salmon and sea-trout, and is fairly abundant in most British salmon rivers. Its specific distinctions vary greatly with local conditions, so much so, sometimes, as almost to make it past recognition. Grey-trout is one of its provincial names, round-tail another, and on the north-east coast it is known as the scurf. So much does the bull-trout resemble the true salmon in appearance, that, after the tail has been clipped square, it is sold as such. This resemblance between· the two species extends to haunt and habit, food, spawning, and migration. The bull-trout attains to a considerable weight ; and just as the fish is in good condition or otherwise, so its flesh is pink or yellowish white. As a game-fish, it affords capital sport, and fights as vigorously as the salmon or brown-trout.

TROUT.

OF all fresh-water fishes the brown brook-trout
is the one best loved by the angler. Salmon,
trout, and grayling, are the aristocrats of the waters,
and constitute the game-fishes of Britain. The
rivers and streams which they haunt lead us to
the finest and wildest scenery—for only the pure
sparkling waters are congenial to them. Every
one loves running water, and there is a strange
fascination about it difficult to define. Men direct
their roads by the waterways, and for reasons far
other than those of trade and commerce. Only
the angler fully knows what these reasons are, and
he it is who sees a hundred sights and hears a
hundred sounds which are hidden from the
traveller on the dusty highway. Flogging the
trout-streams in spring, is surely the most fascinating pastime in which man may indulge, and
truly blessed is he who has the opportunity. The
trout-fisher cannot but be a minute philosopher—
" He must, he is, he cannot but be wise." This is

how Shakespeare described his Antiquary, and has not the author of "*I go a-fishing*" taught us that there is much in common between the angler and the antiquary?   How shall we look at the trout ; how review his history ; and how, further, forge some description of that "cold, sweet, silvery life, wrapped in round waves, and quickened with touches of transporting fear"? Others have begun at the beginning.

Of late years it has been our duty to patiently watch and study the fish on their spawning-beds ; and if ever trout-streams are more interesting than when the March-brown and the May-fly are "on," surely it is now.   Look where we will, the fish are heading up-stream to their spawning-grounds.   The salmon leaves the teeming seas, and the trout his river reaches, for the tributaries. At this time, the fish glide through the deep water with as much eagerness as they rushed down the same river as silvery samlets or tiny trout. Maybe they will stay at some well-remembered pool ; but the first frosts remind them that they must seek the shallower waters.   A brown spate rolling down is another potent reminder, as they know that by its aid rocks and weirs will be more easily crossed.   If their accustomed waterways are of solid foam, they get up easily ; but soft spray gives them little hold.   We must surmount

all obstacles, however, and hurry on to the bright
brooks and pebbly shallows. The "redds" are
selected where the streams are clearest and purest,
where gravel prevails without the presence of
sediment. It is interesting to watch the fish settle
down to their domestic duties, and now much of
their ordinary watchfulness seems to leave them.
Although this facilitates observation, it also assists
the fish-poacher in his nefarious task. When the
female trout has scooped out a hole with her snout,
she deposits the eggs at intervals in the sand.
Whilst this is proceeding, with what care and
attention her lord attends her! See how he rises
and falls, now passing over, now under, and
settling first upon this side, then upon that.
Observe, too, how he drives off the young and
unfertile fish which are ever lying in wait to
devour the spawn. When the "milt" has been
fertilised, the whole is covered over, there to
remain till the eggs are hatched. The quantity
of spawn deposited is such as to suggest that
nothing which man could do would have any
appreciable influence; and this is more readily
understood when it is known that a trout deposits
one thousand eggs, and a salmon upwards of nine
hundred, for every pound of their live weight. In
this connection, however, a vast number of enemies
have to be taken into account. A single ill-timed

spate will destroy millions of eggs by tearing them from the gravel, and a whole host of aquatic enemies have to be reckoned with. And this, it must be borne in mind, before the fish are hatched. The swan alone is able to destroy a gallon of spawn a day, and it is aided by other aquatic birds.

The process of hatching is long ; but ultimately the eggs hatch into avelins. These at first lurk in any quiet retreat, though as soon as the yolk-sac is absorbed, they begin to feed, and are termed fry. Until this period they derive their nutriment from the yolk, and absorb only as much oxygen as will support life. The fry sink into the sheltering gravel, get under little rests, and only venture out as they see the tiniest bits of animal food floating down. If the embryo troutlets had enemies whilst still in the egg, they have more now. Fry afford delicate morsels to predatory water insects, to grebes, ducks, kingfishers, herons, and to every mature fish that haunts the stream. These have all to be reckoned with, and the fry have a hard time of it. By this time they have attained to an inch in length, and are daily better able to look after themselves. As they awake to their active summer life, the troutlets find themselves far up the tributaries ; and here they will remain until they descend to the main waters. This will be in from ten to sixteen months.

When they have dropped down to the great river, they are chary of venturing far out into the world of waters, but for a time haunt the gravel-beds, preferring those with little bays and eddies. The pebbly reaches afford them the greatest protection; and the more thickly grown are the banks with brambles and cresses the better. The first bring food; the second afford protection. Fry are usually found in about four inches of water, and the tendency is for the fish to get into deeper conditions as they increase in age and size. They always exhibit sufficient instinct, however, to remain near those spots which would enable them to get into quiet eddies, so as not to be swept away by the rushing waters. When the fish descend the streams they have attained to three or four inches in length, and are known as "yearlings." This is a generally de-scriptive term, though not always accurate. The troutlets have now attained to a stage when they can begin the battle of life, and although they have fewer they have larger enemies. Herons destroy quantities of yearlings, pike consume great numbers, and we have seen a pair of king-fishers feeding their newly-fledged young upon them. Otters do but little harm to trout at this

c

stage, preferring as they pass up the shallow streams the abundant fresh-water crayfish.

At this stage of their growth troutlings are exceedingly interesting ; and probably every angler has watched them in early summer, when myriads of black gnats revolve just over the water, gambolling in the most frolicsome fashion. At the end of two seasons the young trout have increased to six or eight inches, and at this stage the angler first becomes acquainted with them. Like smelt, they are exceedingly troublesome. The progression from troutlet to trout may be said to take place from the second spring to the end of summer. The fish, which has now attained to half-a-pound in weight, feeds on the various members of the Ephemeræ, grows rapidly, and shakes off its enemies. And now having followed the troutlet from egg to fuller life, we must go back for a moment to the fish that produced it. When trout are spawning but little food is taken, and that from the bottom. As the fish leave the "redds" they are lean and lank, more nearly resembling a pike than a trout. In an ordinary season the fish are all off the redds by December.

It is not until March that trout leave their dark retreats and begin to feed on the surface flies that the first fine days find upon the stream. If the season is open food is abundant, though

the fish rise only for an hour or so in the middle
of the day. Every month brings its own peculiar
insect host, and the trout-angler, observing these,
dresses his flies accordingly. The different nature
of rivers influences not only the supply of insect
food, but the fish. The trout of slow, southern
streams grow quicker and heavier than those of
the colder northern ones. Speaking generally,
the small-winged flies are taken during the day,
the larger-winged ones at night. The trout, like
other fish and some birds, does not swallow its
insect food until a considerable pellet has been
collected in the mouth. The weather influences
the distribution of fish in a river, especially trout.
And this remark applies to the different heights
of the water. A good trout-angler always knows
just where to find his game, not only as to season,
but as to wind and weather. In the cold of
winter, so in summer, the fish are found in the
deep dubs, and a favourite haunt in spring and
summer is upon the "draws" and rippling reaches.
At flood-time the fish are driven to the stream-
sides, worms and food being washed there; and
then they have an aversion to be in rushing,
turbulent, or muddy water. Of course, trout are
found in tarns, ponds, lochs, as well as in rivers;
but the latter they love and thrive in best.
Every one knows what a handsome fish the pink-

spotted trout is, and also that it greatly varies in colour. Trout have the power to take on themselves the colour of the stream which they haunt, and no fresh-water fish conforms more admirably to its environment. This is one of the most remarkable traits in the fish's economy. Other local conditions greatly affect the species. Those in lakes attain to a considerable size, and their predatory instincts are greatly developed. The fact of trout interbreeding with salmon has been already mentioned, as has also the fact of the fertility of the produce. Trout are subject to the same devastating disease as salmon, and of late years several of the best trout-streams in the country have been almost depopulated by its agency.

GRAYLING.

At the present time the Grayling is receiving more attention than perhaps any other of our fresh-water fishes. It is, moreover, in the transition stage, and is about to take rank as one of the "game" fishes of Britain. Then a whole volume by an eminent specialist has been devoted to the setting forth of its merits; and soon it is hoped that the grayling will occupy the status which salmon, trout, and char do now.

The grayling is one of the non-migratory Salmonidæ, and although abundant in certain streams, its distribution as compared with trout is extremely local. To get a good notion of the beauty of the fish, it should be examined in early November. Then it is in its prime, and a typical specimen will show a small head, lozenge-shaped eye, thick shoulders, and a gradual taper to the caudal fin. In colour the fish is dark velvety on the back; sides having rich bloom, shot with purplish copper; belly silver-white.

The large dorsal fin has a line of red-brown spots, and the sides indistinct lines of dark gray. The grayling has a smell peculiar to itself, likened to that of thyme by some, as resembling cucumber by others. This characteristic is repeated in *Thymallus vulgaris*, the technical name of the species.

Unlike trout, grayling do not thrive in mountain streams, but in rivers having a happy combination of ripple and pool, with clean, gravelly bottoms. Their favourite haunts are still streams and eddies, rapid shallows, and gravelly basins. At times the fish are fond of lying at the tail of a weed; and deep water beneath a hollowed bank is a sure "find" when fish are rising freely. When the water is high and discoloured, they are on the edge of the stream, on the look-out for bottom food, but not refusing to rise at a tinselled or highly-coloured fly. The grayling's food consists of flies, larvæ, crustacea, and worms. In spinning for trout in April and May, grayling are occasionally taken with the minnow; but in this case they probably get hooked in driving a supposed intruder from their spawning ground. At all events it is a question whether a minnow has ever been found inside a grayling. The time of spawning is greatly dependent upon the season, but is usually towards the end of April or early in

May. The ova are smaller than those of trout, and are opal-coloured. The young fish hatch in about fifteen days, the period for trout ova varying from forty to fifty days according to temperature and water supply.

Grayling are not difficult to rise with a fly, but they certainly are to hook. This latter requires a quick eye and a delicate "strike," especially when, as often happens, the fly is taken a few inches below the surface, a ripple or an eddy only betraying the movement. There is no splash, no jump, no swirl as with a trout. The fish is seen to rise straight and rapidly from the bottom, flashing and disappearing with equal speed. Sometimes the gleam of the silvery belly is seen before the fish reaches the fly, when the angler invariably strikes too soon. If not pricked, grayling will rise again and again—seven or eight times, as we have seen, only to be hooked at last. Once hooked, there is a peculiar "wobble" on the surface of the water—a moment when many a good grayling gets rid of the hook. This over, the fish fights gamely, often springing right out of the water. October and November are the best grayling months, though good sport may be had to the end of February, providing there is an absence of "snow broth." Morning and evening are the best times for autumn fly-fishing, though a warm, dull day will keep the fish feeding from light till dark. Midday yields the best fishing in winter. Upon one occasion, after fishing fly all day for four brace of fish, worm was tried at dusk. Precisely the same number was basketed the last quarter of an hour—by far the best fish of the day. This is another illustration of the uncertainty of sport.

The grayling angler is either a fly-fisher, or he practises bottom-fishing. The former uses a whole host of flies, the latter worms, gentles, and grasshoppers. An extensive knowledge of the habits of the fish is needed to practise either successfully, as both have been elevated almost to the level of a fine art. In worm fishing some anglers fish with a fixed float, others with a sliding one. In the latter case the depth need not be continually changed, as the worm will keep on or near the bottom. The edges and eddies of streams should be carefully tried, as also pools and "draws." Grasshopper-fishing is just as deadly in certain rivers as it is unsuccessful in others. The Teme and Swale, respectively, give practical illustration of this remarkable fact. The artificial "grasshopper" (the barb being covered with a gentle or two) is cast into streams, eddies, and deep water, and as soon as it has sunk to the bottom it is raised a few inches and sunk again; every likely place being thoroughly searched by means of this sinking and drawing up. Grayling rise to a very large number of flies, and in dressing his lines the angler is guided by the flies which he sees the fish are taking. In midwinter, when the Ephemeræ are absent, it is difficult to know what to try. Iron-blue, claret and orange-bumbles, grey-palmer, red-spinner, silver-dun, and Wickham are all good flies; though light and dark snipe, dotterel, and hackles have often brought big fish to our pannier. Hampshire fishermen seldom fish with anything but dry-fly, whilst northern anglers are partial to hackle-flies. In the rapid and broken waters of northern streams, the latter represents the appearance of a drowned fly far more truthfully than the upright-winged one of the dry-fly fisher; and on the smooth, deep waters of the south, the dry-fly in turn counterfeits the natural floating-fly better than a hackle would. The practised angler, however, does not rely on any hard-and-fast rule; from the character of the river, he sees at once what is best likely to serve his purpose. He has no absurd prejudice, and even condescends to use the worm when the fish invite him to do so. In fly-fishing the cast should be made across and slightly down-stream, the rod point being brought round as the flies are worked down-stream until they are under the bank ; or, if wading, until immediately below. As the best fish often take the fly under water, it often repays the angler to let the tail-fly sink to three or four inches, especially if a bumble or hackled fly. He should strike gently if the flies appear to stop, at any movement of the water, and invariably before making a fresh cast.

The grayling has been described as the "lady of the waters," which title it well deserves. Its quick, silent rise is particularly graceful, though the elegant movements of the fish are tantalising enough. See the quiet, confident way in which it rises at natural flies, and then the disdain with which it treats your clumsy artifice. It will rise to within an inch of your "correct imitation," even apparently take it, and then with a graceful swirl return to its resting-place. The principal English rivers in which grayling are found are the Teme, Test, Avon, Itchen, Wye, Dove, Derwent, Wharfe, Swale, Costa, and the upper reaches of the Trent. In some of these, accurate observations have been made of the fish in its relation to trout ; though the question as to whether the two species can thrive in the same stream is yet far from settled. The champions of the grayling contend that the question is one of food. Where they are introduced and the stock of trout deteriorates, that is evidence only that the streams are too heavily stocked. Then the fish have been introduced to waters which are specially adapted to them, and naturally the trout suffer. In such case it may be well to have a good grayling-stream rather than poor trout-fishing. Northern rivers do not produce such large grayling as the more slowly running ones of the south. In the Dove a fish of a pound weight or upwards is the exception, whilst fish of two or three pounds are not uncommon in the Test and Itchen, and sometimes a noble four-pounder gladdens the heart of the angler. The extent to which the grayling is appreciated as a "sporting fish" is shown by the fact that northern anglers are endeavouring to have it included in the list of "game" fishes—a transition it thoroughly deserves.

IV

PIKE.

Anent the water-wolf, Izaak Walton says that "the mighty luce, or pike, is taken to be the tyrant, as the salmon is the king, of the fresh waters. It is not to be doubted but that they are bred, some by generation and some not, as namely, of a weed called pickerel-weed, unless learned Gesner be much mistaken; for he says this weed, and other glutinous matter, with the help of the sun's heat in some particular months, and some ponds apted for it by nature, do become pikes. But doubtless divers pikes are bred after this manner, or are brought into some ponds some such other ways as is past man's finding out, of which we have daily testimonies." *

---

* Richard Franks, in his *Northern Memoirs*, attacks Walton for what he has said of the pickerel-weed in the following terms: "When I met him (Izaac Walton) at Stafford, I urged his own argument upon him, that pickerel-weed of itself brings pickerel; which question was no sooner stated but he transmits himself to his authority—viz., Gesner, Dubravius, and Aldrovandus—which I readily opposed, and

It is not often that we find the father of fishers either recording that which he himself has not seen, or facts; but here, for once, he is found tripping—as, indeed, he otherwheres admits, when he throws the proof of the curious "fact" upon the learned Gesner. And still there is a half-truth in the statement, as it is now known that the pike sheds its spawn upon pickerel-weed, to which it adheres. The number of eggs which a pike produces is enormous, and in three individuals Buckland found respectively 43,000, 224,640, and 292,300 eggs in fish weighing 35 lbs., 24 lbs., and 28 lbs. respectively. The first of these

offered my reasons to prove contrary; asserting that pickerels have been fished out of ponds where that weed (for aught I know) never grew since the nonage of time, nor pickerel never known to have shed their spawn there. This I propounded from a rational conjecture of the Heronshaw, who, to commode herself with the fry of fish, because in a great measure part of her maintenance, probably might lap some spawn about her legs, in regard to adhering to the segs and bullrushes, near the shallows, where the fish shed their spawn, as myself and others, without curiosity, have observed. And this slimy substance adhering to her legs, etc., and she mounting the air for another station, in all probability mounts with her. Where note, the next pond she haply arrives at, possibly she may leave the spawn behind her; which my Compleat Angler no longer deliberated, but drops his argument, and leaves Gesner to defend it; so huffed away, which rendered him rather a formal opinionist than a reformed and practical artist, because to celebrate such antiquated records whereby to maintain such an improbable assertion."

measured 3 ft. 10½ in. in length, 2 ft. in girth, and was the largest pike Buckland ever saw. After being spawned, probably only a small proportion of the eggs will ever be hatched, for they are fed upon by a host of aquatic creatures. Although the weed upon which pike spawn affords some shelter, it does not offer sufficient to guard it from many devouring enemies. Among these are pike themselves, and numerous fishes that share the same haunt. Wild fowl feed upon it, and the swan seeks it out as a paradise for her brown cygnets; and it is well known that an adult swan will destroy nearly a gallon of spawn in a day. Then there are the small fry of various fishes that are constantly on the look-out for spawn, in addition to birds, beetles, and numerous water insects, which destroy enormous quantities. Even when successfully hatched, the small pike have a hard time of it during their early career, and unless they can manage to steer clear of their parents and elder acquaintances, they will not long survive. If the water in which pike happen to be is limited, only a few of the largest fish survive; and in restocking, care should be taken that the newly-introduced fish should be somewhat equal in age and size. It has frequently come about that one patriarchal pike has been the only denizen of a pond, having long ago

devoured all its smaller compeers. In fact, this
devouring capacity of the fish, and its great
voracity, are among its chief characteristics. The
writer once saw a large jack swimming about
with a smaller one held crosswise in its jaws,
and has frequently noticed personal combats, with
attempts at gorging, by fish of nearly equal size.
Once in particular was this ferocious quality ex-
hibited, under what might have been thought
unlikely conditions. We had been trolling in a
mountain tarn, and had taken several fish, which
were thrown into the water-covered bottom of an
old, slimy punt. Even in this element one pike
attempted to swallow another of about its own
size, succeeding so far as to get the smaller
fish well into its throat. And it may here be
stated that what once gets impacted into a pike's
maw is not likely to return—not alone by reason
of the ferocity already referred to, but more on
account of the eel-trap-like arrangement of its
fine, formidable teeth. Upon one occasion, two
pike were taken in Loch Tay, the one firmly
impacted in the mouth of the other. The head
of the one was tightly inserted up to the termina-
tion of its gill, and part of the first lower fin was
in the mouth of the larger one. The fish together weighed nineteen pounds. A couple of
pike were taken by a lad in a somewhat similar

position from the Tweed, at Kelso, one half-
swallowed by the other. Both fish were alive;
they were placed in water, when the larger made
two or three attempts to swallow its neighbour.
These fish were forwarded to Buckland; and Dr.
Burton, who sent them, remarked that the lad
who captured them wondered much to see "a
muckle fish wi' twa tails." It is fortunate that
most fish seem to know the character of their
predacious neighbour, and no small fry are
allowed, or care, to go near his haunts—those
that were there originally having long ago entered
its voracious jaws. And such jaws! Well may
the little fish in sheer fright jump right out of the
water, or make for the shallows, where the water-
wolf cannot follow them. To the loach, the tiny
sticklebacks, and the silvery minnows, the pike is
a terrible giant and bugbear. Like most predatory
fishes, his appetite is enormous, and his digestion
quick. He will attack and attempt to swallow
one of his own species almost his equal in weight
and size, which feat we have more than once
witnessed. He is also a great enemy to trout,
and we know one of the best trout-streams in
the country which he has almost depopulated.
He is a difficult enemy to circumvent, his extinction being almost impracticable; but with
many baits and lures he affords good sport to

hundreds of anglers where there are scarcely any other fish, and so we must not be too hard upon him.

Throughout Britain the pike is both common and widely distributed. It occurs not only in canals and reservoirs (in some of which it is extremely abundant), but also in many rivers. Pike love deep, logged water, and when they are found in running streams it is mainly in pools and dams. Sometimes they lie in deep dubs, but always make to the shallows to spawn. The eggs are shed in spring, at which time, of course, the fish is in poor condition, and is generally to be found among weeds, or where the water has backed up into an eddy. As to the food of the pike something has been said already; it will devour almost all species of fresh-water fishes, which it endeavours to gulp down whole. It sometimes catches a tartar in a prickly perch, which, finding itself in the pike's jaws, immediately raises its back fin, when all the efforts which the pike can exert are unable to disgorge it. In addition to a pretty wide range of fish food, the pike disdains neither flesh nor fowl, and sometimes even indulges in carrion. A pike has been known to attempt to swallow a salmon, and it is well authenticated that various species of the young

D

of waterfowl have been taken, and they commonly capture water-voles and rats.

One of the legends attaching to the pike is that it lives to a very great age, but this *is* only a legend. Certain large fish are known to have lived from eight to twelve years, and the facts in this connection are well authenticated. There is a story of a pike having existed for two hundred and sixty-seven years. This was the famous Mannheim pike captured in 1497, and which attained to the enormous length of nineteen feet. It had in its gills a brass ring, upon which was engraved in Greek, " I am the first fish which was placed in this pond by the hand of Frederick II., Governor of the World, on the 5th of October, 1230 "—surely the most marvellous pike on record. Its skeleton is still preserved, and is nearly nineteen feet in length, only it happens to be a compound of *two* individuals, and an examination has shown that several vertebræ have been added. The ring of gilded brass could "enlarge itself by springs "—a highly necessary qualification, all things considered.

There is one thing in the life-history of the pike which has never been clearly proved. This is as to its power of making overland journeys— of changing its haunt, either for food or water. It is said that lately an English gentleman, residing at Antwerp, tested this "fact" by constructing two new ponds, one of which was stocked with pike, and the other with small fresh-water fish. After two days the ponds were emptied, when it was found that some of the pike had made the journey between the two, and had created sad havoc among their neighbours. This experiment, however, could hardly be taken as offering conclusive evidence of the truth of the "fact" it was intended to demonstrate. The habit of pike sunning themselves on the top of the water and their going in pairs is well known.

V

PERCH.

THE armoured perch is certainly one of the handsomest of British fresh-water fishes. He is a bold biter, too, and affords sport to a whole army of anglers who have never flogged a trout-stream or fished a salmon river. His distribution is almost as wide as that of the Englishman, and he is as hardy as prolific. A large female fish will yield two hundred thousand eggs in a season, and as these hatch rapidly, the possible increase of the species may be imagined. Perch-fry, however, have an army of aquatic enemies, which allow but a small number ever to reach maturity. There is a quiet confidence about the perch which renders observation of its habits both easy and interesting. If fed by hand they soon recognise their friend, and are punctual in their appearing. Looking down into the still, deep water, the first sign of the approach of perch is the sudden stampede of a shoal of silvery roach. The metallic scales of these flash in the sunlight;

though the perch conform more nearly to their environment. The reflection of the leaves and the waving of the weeds cause the water to be dark olive-green, and before the "bass" rise to the warmer water it is difficult to detect them in the deeps. As they approach the surface, their easy evolutions and bright colouring are at once seen. The burnished armour is deep bronze, done with bars of darker green, the whole shaded by a sheen of peacock iridescence. The fins show as sparks of fire in the dark water, and alternately the dorsal spine is erected and depressed. Perfect amity seems to exist betwixt the perch and his neighbours—so long as he is allowed "to rule the roast." If a roach or gudgeon so much as attempt to invade his feeding-ground, he loses not a moment in preparing his weapons. It has been well said that the armament of spines on a perch's back acts as the index of his mind; and the conceit recommends itself to any one who has observed the fish in its haunts. Just as the smaller birds drop into their leafy retreats at the shadow of a hawk, so the small fry of the waters rush to their rests at the green glint of the "water-wolf." Not so, however, the perch. He parades himself before the pike, at the same time erecting his spiny armour. Not only pike, but other predatory fish, and grebes, have been found choked by armoured perch and sticklebacks.

The salmon- or trout-fisher is rarely averse to devote a day to perch. In fact, this is the game at which he was "entered," and he has never quite forgotten that first golden afternoon. He remembers every bait which will tempt the prettily-finned fish to drag down the float, and has used them all. How many hours has he stood by the bank of some sluggish stream or quiet tarn, every moment of which was filled with pleasurable hope? And then the intense excitement of hauling one of the crimson-tinted fishes on to the bank, and how this was re-peated again and again until the perch stopped "biting." But to hundreds of others besides the youthful enthusiast, this beautiful fish has given quiet, pleasurable enjoyment; and then, is he not one of the very best-known of all our "sporting fishes"? Through the long hours of a sunny summer day, the perch will sometimes continue to feed; and then the catch may be counted by the score. But oftener the conditions are not nearly so favourable, and then the fish may severely try the long-suffering patience of the angler.

"'Ad e'er a bite, Jim?" "No, I only cum here yesterday morning." This is an apt though exaggerated illustration of the degradation to which the float fisher may occasionally be brought. Anglers try to lure the perch with a great variety of mysterious compounds, but usually the most successful is a small red-worm. This should be allowed to rise and fall, for the apparent animation of the prey invariably excites the fish to come at the bait with a rush. Immature perch bite recklessly, larger ones much more circumspectly. There are certain climatic conditions, however, when almost every fish of a shoal may be bagged. The dark, golden shadows pass and re-pass beneath ; though immediately a bait touches the water every fish rushes towards it. The wide-open mouth, the flashing fins, the erect dorsal spines—all show irritation when the worm is withdrawn. If the tactics are changed, and a perch is hooked, he fights not ungamely, though he sometimes succeeds in shaking himself free. If, however, he is landed, his fate in no way intimidates his neighbours ; they come, one by one, until the last of the shoal is lying among the docks and nettles. More frequently the big fish are slow to be thus lifted out, though the smaller ones seem to have no such clear objection.

In Windermere and Derwentwater, perch are exceedingly abundant, and sometimes hundreds are taken from a boat in a single evening's fishing. But where they exist in such quantities they are usually of small size. Thousands of perch are also to be found in Slapton Ley, Devonshire; though the largest and best are to be found in the Avon, Kennet, and the Norfolk Broads. The economy of the perch is somewhat difficult to comprehend. Being so exceedingly prolific, they sometimes exist in thousands. When this is the case the "schools" invariably consist of the smallest fish. Only large ones are to be had where the species is numerically weak, and hence the best fishing is to be had in preserved waters. The only way to improve an existing stock is to reduce it by two-thirds, then to feed the remainder. Unlike some of the coarse fish, the perch rarely attains to any size, and whilst it is not uncommon to read of individuals of six, seven, or eight pounds, yet a two-pound perch is a large and handsome fish. Buckland took casts of perch of 3 lbs. 2 ozs. and 2 lbs. 11 ozs., the former containing 127,240 eggs, the latter 155,620. Whilst perfectly wild fish rarely attain to this size, it is not difficult to produce larger ones under semi-artificial conditions.

A stretch of water known to the writer runs along the edge of an old English garden. The fish are encouraged to congregate along its sides, and they show quite an amount of confidence in coming to be fed. Coots and dabchicks breed among the reeds, and both fight with the fish for possession of the soft-bodied food. In hot weather the perch swim near the surface, and then the aquatic birds have no chance against them. As a red-worm reaches the water, every fish rushes up, and sometimes a dozen open mouths reach the morsel at the same instant. If absolute possession has not been gained, there is a struggle, and the pool is lashed into quite a fishy commotion. The jaws are at work, the red fins flash like sparks of fire, and the bronze bodies seem all over the pool at once. There is an old pile which they love to haunt, and they are sometimes seen to gently rub their sides against it. In sharp contrast to the dusky perch are the silvery roach. These describe their graceful evolutions just on the side of the "Perch-pool," but rarely invade it; if they do, the perch at once become aggressive, and the "water-sheep" are not long in making good their retreat. We have frequently taken large fish of both species from this preserve with fly. A quick eye and hand is requisite to successful fly-fishing for perch, and once indulged, it becomes quite a fascinating pursuit—how fascinating the following incident will show. A "gentleman poacher" of the neigh-

bourhood made a wager that he would bring to
bank every one of a school of seventeen perch on
a single evening. The bet was taken, and the
feat was accomplished with only two lures—red-
worms and a half worn-out trout-fly. It may be
added that every fish was returned to the hole evidently none the worse for its night's adventure.

There is occasionally another night denizen of
the old "Perch-hole," which as an expert even
out-poaches the poacher. We take our place by
the stream-side and breathlessly wait. A faint
whistle, unlike that of any bird, comes up-stream,
and the dark water is moved. Trout cease to
rise; the whistle comes nearer, and then a rustle
is heard. The osier-beds are visibly stirred, and
some long, dark object makes its way between
the parted stems. A movement would dispel the
dark shadow. The rustle among the withy wands
is repeated again and again, and now we know
that the young otters have left their impregnable
rocky bank, and are following their dam. She
has reconnoitred, and all is safe. Paddling down-
stream come two objects, and, arriving at the
pool, stop, tumble and frolic, rolling over and
over, and round and round, and performing the
most marvellous evolutions. They swing on a
willow spray, and dash with lightning rapidity at
a piece of floating bark, tumble with it, wrestle

with it, and go through a hundred graceful movements; then are motionless, then begin to play,
and so continue for nearly an hour, when, as if
suddenly alarmed, they rush down-stream to their
feeding-grounds. Fishing is continued through
the darkness, until, in the dewy meadow, another
sound comes up the wind, and the deep, sonorous
voice of an otter-hound breaks into the fairy-like
dawn scene.

VI

ROACH AND RUDD.

I HAVE just been indulging in an hour's delicious laziness, dreamily watching a shoal of silvery-sided roach rising and falling towards the warm sunlight. It is hard to understand why anglers should call the roach a "coarse" fish, as he is a very *Beau Brummel* of the waters. Coarse he may be as compared with salmon and trout, but in no other sense. The character of the fish in the water is in keeping with his aristo-cratic appearance out of it. All his movements are slow and studied. Whatever he does he does gracefully. He is never in a hurry, and rarely commits himself. Isaak Walton says you may take notice that, as the carp is accounted the water-fox for cunning, so the roach is ac-counted the water-sheep for his simplicity or foolishness. For our part, we have never found the roach as stupid as he is reputed. Let your float be too big or too brightly coloured, too near the bottom or the top, your bait not to his taste, and you will find that he can be even hypercritical upon occasion. He will swim above it or below it, he will swim round and round it, only at last to be disgusted at its clumsiness, to give a delicate wave of his tail, and glide gracefully away. And then the roach of my acquaintance are like those of an eminent Frenchman—inclined to controversy, indecisive in conclusions. Sometimes they will bite, sometimes they will not ; one never knows the reason why. To catch him the fisherman must have a subtle eye and a steady hand. One should take all sorts of precautions, for if he is curious, he is also at the same time excessively suspicious, and to catch him, one must use the finest possible tackle.

The spot from which I watch my shoal of roach is half buried in lush summer grass, so that while I can see the fish, they cannot see me. All their movements are the very poetry of motion, and the shoal seem to act by some subtle, hidden impulse. They occupy a deep pool in a trout-stream, and as the anglers complain that they destroy the ground-food of the trout for eight months of the year, we have set about catching them. The small fry of their kind are easily taken in quantity, and to these the title of " water-sheep" may be apt enough. An angler has to put forth all his wiles to get round the bigger fish, but by exercising a little patience, he may overcome all their idiosyncrasies. After our experiences, we must admit that the roach is a delicate fish to circumvent, always supposing that he has attained to any size. But once on the bank, there is no gainsaying his beauty as he flops out his life among the docks and nettles. The fish are just clean and bright from spawning, and this is how they show: Back and upper parts of a delicate weedy green, flashing and glowing with metallic lustre ; these colours pale as they approach the medial line, and then turn silver, which passes into white on the under parts ; the back and tail fins stand out sharply in dull red, the anal and ventral fins glowing with crimson. These, with a symmetrical body, and a tiny, " blood-like " head turned into broad shoulders, complete the picture of a handsome fish. As much cannot be said of the edible qualities of the roach as for his gentlemanly appearance, though he has his champions in this respect too, only he requires to be daintily done in the cooking.

The roach is a fish of many waters, and seems peculiarly adapted to various environments. He is at home in sluggish streams with muddy bottoms, though his colours become a little dulled ; here, too, in this clear tarn, high on the hills, he lives in contentment with the trout and rudd. In our trout-stream proper (whence we are trying to rid him) he seems particularly happy, only he steers clear of the rushing water, and quietly allows himself to drop down to where the water is "logged." In addition to these situations, he may frequently be found in ponds, reservoirs, and even in river estuaries only a few miles above the sea. The regular haunts of the roach, however, are sluggish rivers; and the stiller reaches of the Thames produce some magnificent fish. London roach-anglers are said to excel all others, and it is even asserted that they have reduced the patient trade to a fine art— how fine only the initiated know. Roach spawn in May and June, and in the Thames shoals of them may be seen making their way to the higher reaches, in search of suitable water-weed. Upon this the spawn is deposited, and so engrossed do they become in the act that their dorsal fins often show above the surface. The reproductive powers of the roach are enormous, and a matured fish may deposit as many as 480,000 eggs. When spawning is over the shoals drop down to the pebbly bottoms to scour themselves, and are in good condition in a remarkably short time after returning to the deeps. They will then rise to the fly like trout,

but this does not last long, and by far the best
bait are gentles (especially those of the blue-
bottle), or paste mixed with cotton-wool.

In our mind's eye there is at this moment a
favourite "dub," where, in bygone years, we
used to capture fish of great size and numbers,
which were supposed to be roach. They turned
out, however, to be Rudd, "red-eyes" as the
old poachers called them. Walton was not
at all sure of the rudd, and thought it was
a kind of bastard roach ; and he remarks that
the Thames, below London Bridge, affords the
"largest and fattest" in this "nation." According
to the knowledge of his times, these red fish
were produced by bream and roach mixing their
eggs and milt together, and although they became numerous, they never grew to any great
size. This is quite erroneous. At this moment
a brace of magnificent monsters are lying before
me, and of all coarse fish, surely they must be
the handsomest. They have only been out of
the water a couple of hours, are in the pink of
condition, and just turn the scale at four pounds.
And this is how they came by their death. We
were searching for coot's eggs among the reeds
of a mountain tarn, when two or three big fish
began to rise from the warm, shallow bank. A
single hair-line was quickly tied, and the end fly

dropped quietly among the shoal. There was a
faint show of concentric rings in the water, then
a mad plunge, and a ten minutes' fight. The
single strand of hair held out bravely, and a
glorious rudd was pulled aboard, much to the
excitement of the girls and dogs. It was a
deep, handsome fish, with red eyes; cheek and
gills golden yellow, this darkening to blue and
green on the back; sides bright coppery, golden
below; belly tinged with pink, and shot with
metallic lustre; all the fins red; the body
suddenly narrowing towards the tail, which is
deeply indented. One of the characteristics of
the rudd is its tenacity of life, fish sometimes
showing signs of life after having been out of
the water twelve hours. During the day the
rudd lies in the deepest part of its haunt, making
for the shallows at morning and evening. At
the former time it is a ground-feeder; but
when it rises from the deeper water it takes flies
from the surface. We came to the knowledge
of this fact after a somewhat heated experience.
After fishing all day and taking nothing save a few
small roach, the sun got behind a dark thunder-
cloud, when the rudd immediately commenced to
rise. As twilight increased the mere seemed
everywhere broken by bubbles, and this time,
equipped with flies dressed on fine gut, the

E

slaughter that ensued was great. That long summer evening was a memorable one, and in weight it proved the best fishing of a life-time. The larger fish fought pluckily, but as there was no method in their madness, they were pulled in one by one. Yet what is the " play " of a hundredweight of coarse rudd to that of a ten-pound salmon fresh run from the sea ? But are not comparisons odious ? A long day in the old slimy punt has its quiet joys as well as one after salmon and trout ; and then each can be indulged in when the other is prohibited.

VII

CARP AND BREAM.

THERE are no indigenous British carp. Carp-culture was once not uncommon in England under semi-domestic conditions, though most of the fish that now inhabit our ponds and rivers have been introduced from the Continent. The first mention of the carp is that by Dame Juliana Berners, in the "*Boke of St. Albans*," printed by Wynkyn de Worde, at Westminster, in 1496. In this it is described as a "deyntous fysshe, but scarce"—which we may well believe; for more than a century later Leonard Mascall takes to himself the credit of having introduced this fish into English waters. As fish stews are found in connection with almost every religious house throughout the country, and as many of these are specially adapted to carp-culture, doubtless these fish were introduced and tended by monks. The fish of the carp kind found most commonly in Britain are the Common carp (*Cyprinus carpis*); the Crucian or Prussian carp (*Cyprinus gilelio*);

and the Golden carp, or gold-fish (*Cyprinus
auratus*). As already stated, these have all been
introduced ; but as carp in general are tenacious
of life even under adverse circumstances, the fish
have thriven amazingly in their naturalised haunts.
By far the most common of the carp is the first-
named, which occurs generally in ponds, and has
even found its way into several rivers. The
crucian carp occurs less abundantly, whilst the
gold variety is rarer still. In many parts of the
country this occurs in reservoirs of warm water
connected with manufactories — the hot steam
driven into the water making it peculiarly congenial to the gold-fish.

" The Carp is the queen of rivers ; a stately,
a good, and a very subtle fish, that was not at
first bred, nor hath been long in England, but is
now naturalised. . . . The carp, if he have
water room and good feed, will grow to a very
great bigness and length ; I have heard to be much
above a yard long. It is said by Jovius, who hath
writ of fishes, that in the lake Lurian, in Italy,
carps have thriven to be more than fifty pounds
weight. Gesner says a carp has been known
to live in the Palatinate above a hundred years ;
but most conclude, that, contrary to pike or luce,
all carp are the better for age and bigness. The
tongues of carps are noted to be choice and costly

meat, especially to them that buy them; but
Gesner says carps have no tongues like other fish,
but a piece of flesh-like fish in their mouth like a
tongue, and should be called a palate; but it is
certain it is choicely good; and that the carp is to
be reckoned amongst those leather-mouthed fish,
which I told you have their teeth in their throat,
and for that reason he is very seldom lost by
breaking his hold if your hook be once stuck in
his chaps. . . . I will proceed to give you some
observations of the carp, how to angle for him,
and to dress him, *but not till he is caught.* . . .
and my first direction is, that if you will fish for a
carp, you must put on a very large measure of
patience. . . . and being possessed of that hope
and patience, which I wish to all fishers, especially
to the carp-angler, I shall tell you with what bait
to fish for him."

Were we disposed to preach a sermon on
carp, this advice from the father of fishers would
prove an admirable text. Carp are sluggish fish,
and usually haunt logged water. Common carp
almost live in mud, and as they draw their
sustenance from it, the flesh has generally a
muddy flavour. When carp were commonly kept
in the old fish stews, it was customary before
using them to take out a number and submit them
to the purifying influences of fresh water. This

was done by placing them in a box or cage, which
was deposited in a stream, the fish thereby gaining
in flavour. Culture has done much to improve
the carp, and American pisciculturists have now
so far succeeded as to breed a scaleless variety.
Looking to the fish as a source of food supply,
this is an important step in advance, and the
result has been brought about mainly by careful
selection. Although, as already stated, carp are
found for the most part in ponds, yet they
inhabit rivers, though they avoid all currents,
and seek silted or muddy bottoms. In such case
they are not so prolific as when found in ponds,
and as well as producing fewer eggs, they spawn
less frequently. To prove how prolific, under
favourable circumstances, carp really are, it may
be mentioned that the roe of a fish 21 lbs. in
weight contained 1,310,750 eggs, and another of
16½ lbs. 2,059,750 eggs. There is one matter
anent the breeding of this species which is not
quite clear. Female fish have sometimes three or
four successive layers of eggs, which they would
seem to shed, but at remarkably short intervals.
If the weather is warm, spawning begins in April,
but more commonly in May; even with fish in
the same haunts, and under precisely like conditions, spawning sometimes continues for three
or four months. Temperature affects carp more

than any other fish, and this probably because it
is not an indigenous but an introduced species.
In cold water they spawn but seldom, their fecun-
dity being affected ; the fish are stunted and less
brightly coloured ; whereas in warm water they
live to a considerable age, and attain to a large
size. It is owing to these facts that carp flourish so
much better in the southern than in the northern
parts of Britain.

The food of the carp consists for the most part
of succulent stalks of water-plants, of worms,
insects, and soft-bodied life generally which is
found in mud. In winter they lie in a semi-
dormant condition at the bottom of ponds partially
buried. This does not occur when the water-
temperature is high, as here the fish feed and
thrive through the hardest weather. Carp are
not much fished for, as they can hardly be said to
afford good sport, and then they are most difficult
to circumvent. They possess leather-like mouths,
and there is a barbule at the upper part of each
corner of the mouth. The following interesting
quotation from Lady Colin Campbell's *Book of
the Running Brook and of Still Waters* sets
forth some of the points enumerated above as to
the value of carp-culture, their rate of growth, and
above all, their tenacity of life. This refers to the
highlands of Limousin, and gives a graphic

account of what takes place there every three
years : " All the able-bodied men of the country-
side are engaged for a certain day in October to
meet at one of the ponds, that on the highest
level being taken first. The sluices are opened
three days previously, and the water allowed to
gradually run off, leaving that bed of deep mud
which seems to be one of the necessaries of carp
existence.   When there is only a thin rill of
water left trickling down the centre of the erstwhile pond, the fishing begins.   On all sides the
carp lie floundering, panting, gasping on the
expanse of mud ; in some places they are two
or three deep on top of one another.   Though
the quantity of carp in these ponds is something
extraordinary, they do not seem to suffer indi-
vidually from their great numbers, for the fish are
remarkably fine and heavy.   The men wade
through the mud, catching the carp by the gills,
and flinging them on to the bank.   There they
are weighed by men who have come with carts
from the nearest town to buy the fish, and, after
the weighing, the carp are packed amongst straw
in the carts as tightly as possible.   When the
carts are full, they return to the town, and the
carp are then placed in tanks. A carp takes
a good deal of killing, and though being tightly
packed in straw for a whole day, and jolted down-

hill for perhaps four hours, may strike him as
a novel experience, it does not do him the very
least harm ; as soon as he is released from durance
vile and placed in the tanks, he resumes the even
tenor of his way. . . . While the fishing goes on,
groups of women make fires on the bank, and
they heat cauldrons of soup mixed with strong
red wine, which is served out unceasingly in
bowls to the soaked and muddy fishermen. This
is a necessary precaution in a climate where
people are sometimes snowed up for days early in
November. The gipsy-fires and groups of women,
the men wading through the mud and water,
mostly dressed in frieze coats of the most brilliant
hues, and with high boots to protect them somewhat during their task ; the piles of shining,
glistening fish, and, in the background, the carts
waiting to take away the spoils, altogether make
a highly picturesque scene."

The second naturalised species is the Crucian
or Prussian carp. This and the last are much
alike in haunt, habit, and food. They spawn
somewhat earlier ; but as they rarely bite, and
when they do, yield but little sport, they are
hardly interesting to the angler. The crucian
carp rarely attains to the size of its congener,
the common species, and one of two pounds is
considered a large fish. There is a well-defined

variety of the carp under notice that has sometimes been elevated to the rank of a species ;
but careful examination proves it to be only a
variety after all.

The Golden carp is the third species which has
found its way into Britain. It mostly occurs in
warm mill-ponds, and according to the degree of
temperature so its colouring is sombre or brilliant.
The very poetry of motion may be seen in the
movements of a " school " of golden carp, and as
they are frequently kept in confinement, the sight
is a not unfrequent one. The fish seem quite
to appreciate the care bestowed upon them, and
to reciprocate kindness. Although they rarely
breed when confined within a limited space,
yet they do so prolifically in open warm water,
and in this respect show that they can stand
varying degrees of temperature.

" The Bream, being at full growth, is a large
and stately fish. He will breed both in rivers and
ponds ; but loves best to live in ponds, and
where, if he likes the water and air, he will grow
not only to be very large, but as fat as a hog.
He is by Gesner taken to be more pleasant or
sweet than wholesome. This fish is long in
growing, but breeds exceedingly in a water that
pleases him ; yea, in many ponds, so fast as to
over-store them, and starve the other fish.

Gesner reports that in Poland a certain and a great number of large breams were put into a pond, which, in the next following winter, was frozen up into one entire ice, and not one drop of water remaining, nor one of these fish to be found, though they were diligently searched for ; and yet, next spring, when the ice was thawed, and the weather warm, and fresh water got into the pond, he affirms they all appeared again. This Gesner affirms, and I quote my author because it seems almost as incredible as the resurrection of an atheist ; but it may win something, in point of believing it, to him that considers the breeding or renovation of the silkworm and of many insects."—WALTON.

The Bream is close cousin to the carp, and, like its congeners, loves large stretches of water. All the members of this family do best in comparatively still water, and when their environment is suitable, they grow and multiply exceedingly. In winter they lie in the " deeps," but in summer come to the warmer water-strata near the surface. They swim in shoals, and at this time the back fin is often apparent above the water. A " school " of bream is an exceedingly pretty sight, and after a hot day, they frequently indulge in evolutions, just, as it would seem, for the love of the enjoyment. They are rather omnivorous feeders,

and by no means confine themselves to one
class of diet. They are fond of minute animal
organisms, worms, larvæ, beetles, snails, and at
certain times they feed upon water-weeds. In
summer they rise well to several small flies,
though they prove rather a dead weight at the
end of a line. Red-worms furnish the best
general bait; but a great variety of ingredients is
used for ground-baiting. When once a shoal of
fish has been attracted, it is difficult to alarm them,
and the fate of one member has often no deterrent
effect upon the rest. Spawning takes place in
April and May, and the number of ova in a single
fish has been known to number 100,000. Seeing
this, it is easy to understand the rate at which the
species reproduces itself under anything like
favourable circumstances. The bream grows
rapidly, and on account of its good qualities it
was much kept in stews in connection with the
religious houses of the past. The fish so kept
must have been specially tended and fed, and
those of the present day would hardly justify the
once popular proverb to the effect that, " The man
who had bream in his pond was able to bid
his friend welcome." By skilful cooking, bream
at their best can be made palatable, especially
at a time in autumn when they leave the mud and
weeds to feed almost exclusively upon delicate

ephemeræ. Fly-fishing for bream can certainly
be recommended, as it affords a decidedly lively
change to the more patient methods frequently
pursued.

"The Chub has the same fault as the York-
shireman's horse—he is bad to catch, and no good
when caught." Such is the character given to
this, another cousin of the carp. Although perhaps not the best comparison to institute, the
chub in its habits somewhat resembles the char.
Like that fish it stays at the bottom of its haunt
in winter, rising to the warmer water in summer.
It is withal a shy and wary fish, and the successful
chub-angler must be a subtle fisher indeed. Just
as the larger trout, screened by overhanging
boughs, lie in the shady holes in summer, waiting for insect food, so does the chub. And this
habit has suggested the same mode of fishing for
the two species. The trout is "dibbed" for with
a bluebottle-fly, and the chub is quite unable to
resist a cockchafer. "Dibbing" consists of fishing with a bait at the end of a short line, from
some tree or overhanging rock, the bait barely
touching the water; and in this way very large
fish are often taken. Great care has to be
exercised, however, as no liberties can be taken
with chub. An unusual shadow, the sight of rod
or line, will each drive down the shoal to the cool

depths, and once driven away the fish are slow in returning.

The diet of the chub consists of insects, worms, and larvæ, and it takes a good deal of its food from the surface. Fish of from two to three pounds are not uncommon, and individuals have been known to attain to four and five pounds in weight. Spawning takes place during the earlier spring months on the shallower portions of the chub's haunts, and at this time the fish are much less shy than ordinarily. The chub may be said to be generally distributed in the south, becoming rarer in the northern counties. It affects rivers that have deep, shaded holes, and is rarely or never found upon rocky beds or in quickly running water.

VIII

BARBEL, DACE, AND GUDGEON.

> In they went, and hunted about,
> Open-mouthed like chub or trout,
> And some with upper lip thrust out,
> Like that fish for routing—the barbel.

BUCKLAND was fond of quoting these lines, and the subject of them he calls a water-pig, as its habits in the water so much resemble those of a pig on land. But whilst this is so, it must not be taken that the barbel is a foul-feeding fish, as in this respect it is cleaner than many of its congeners. Worms form the chief portion of its diet, and for these it loves to "rout" with its snout against gravelly banks or clumps of protruding earth. Like the silvery roach, the barbel feeds much at night, and may almost be said to be nocturnal in its habits. The fish has its name from six barbules that depend from its lower and upper jaws. Just as a cat's sensitive whiskers aid it in its night wanderings, so these barbules doubtless aid

their possessor in obtaining its food in its dark
retreats.   All anglers must have noticed that
the barbel is most active at morning and evening,
and it is at these times that the best takes are
had.   At dusk they issue forth and usually plant
themselves where their retreat is narrowed, and
there wait for anything that is washed down.
When light comes, they make back to their dark
recess, and both feed less, and are more inactive
than during the night.   In winter, barbel stay
almost wholly in their dark retreats, and get into
very low condition.   Their ordinary food consists
of worms, the fry of coarse fish, and minute forms
of aquatic life generally.   An enormous number
of eggs are deposited in May and June, and these
are jealously guarded by the parents.   After the
spawn is thrown down, both male and female
work assiduously in covering it with sand ; this is
done for protective reasons, and as the work is
progressing, the spawners drive away every fish
that dares to venture near.   The eggs are hatched
in about a fortnight, and if the weather be warm,
the fry are soon able to shift for themselves.
The barbel sometimes attains to ten pounds in
weight, and one of fifteen pounds is known to
have been taken.   The barbules on the head of
the fish detract somewhat from its personal appearance, but it is, withal, fairly handsome.   The

upper parts are copper-green, having a decided bronze lustre; under parts white, irides golden yellow; and the mouth a reddish flesh-colour. A medial line runs along the body. In certain rivers the barbel is fairly abundant, though from the nature of its haunts, its distribution is somewhat local.

The dace must not be omitted from our list of sporting fishes. It shuns polluted streams, as also those with quickly flowing water; and is found in greatest abundance in rivers that have deep, clear pools. It will rise to the fly, and in this way quite good takes are often to be had when the fish are feeding upon winged food. Dace more than other fish love to wanton in the streams which they haunt, especially in warm weather. They swim in shoals, and if observed with the sun upon them present quite a pretty sight. Ever and anon one of them turns its silvery sides uppermost, and sometimes the stream seems to flash with their silver. Buckland has said: "The dace has the vivacity of the bleak and the swagger of the chub, and that therefore it requires some little attention to catch him." This is quite true, unless he is in the humour to be caught—which is seldom. He may easily be netted, however, but netting in this connection generally savours of poaching. Except roach, no fish makes such bait for pike,

F

and in this capacity the dace is sometimes used for trout. The success of the fish as a live bait is probably owing to the silvery sheen of its flashing sides. The dace is small, and rarely attains to more than nine inches in length. I have spoken of the fish as taking the fly; but Walton recommends that it should be fished for with paste made from a " pure fine manchet." And then he wisely adds, that when you fish with it you must have a small hook, a quick eye, and a nimble hand, or the bait is lost, and the fish, too — if one may lose that which he never had. " With this paste you may, as I said, take both the roach and the dace or dare, for they be much of a kind in matter of feeding, cunning, goodness, and usually in size. And therefore take this general direction for some other baits that may concern you to take notice of. They will bite almost at any fly, but especially at ant-flies."

The gudgeon is a gregarious fish, usually swimming in shoals, and found in rivers and streams having gravelly beds. Among the stones and pebbles the little fish love to rummage, and here they obtain their food. The parts of the shallow streams which they best love to haunt are where the water is "thin" and rippling, or the " reaches" between deep dubs. Although gudgeon are partial to fresh streams, they also inhabit ponds and canals, especially those which receive drainage or surface-water from the land. And in such situations, where these runners are found, the fish may often be observed feeding at their mouths. A shoal so engaged affords a pretty sight, especially if the water be clear and has the sun upon it. It is at such times that gudgeon are seen at their best. They are exceedingly lively, rushing hither and thither like streaks of silver light—the fish crossing and recrossing, but never for a moment remaining in one position. The surface-water from fields brings down a quantity of various lower forms of life, and upon these gudgeon feed. The little fishes are omnivorous in their appetites, and devour tiny red-worms (which they love well), insects and their larvæ, small shelled-snails, water-beetles, and spawn. But although such greedy feeders, they are not particular in their diet, and the water surrounding a certain sewage-farm known to us swarms with them. Sewage in solution seems not to affect them, and they frequently feed upon the foulest matter flowing from pipes. Anent this, Buckland writes of gudgeon as follows : " To lawyers, the poor innocent gudgeon may be a very serviceable fish, for he may be brought as a witness into court, to prove that pollutions are not injurious to salmon or trout fisheries. A live gud-

geon is placed, in the presence of the Judge and
jury, in the polluted water, and he does not 'turn
up,' therefore the counsel argues that manufactories
or the town sewer are not in fault, as the water
allowed to flow into the river is not injurious to
fish life. If an expert in fishery matters does not
happen to be present, this gudgeon argument
will go down, as the Judge and jury probably are
not aware that gudgeon are very fond of living in
sewer-water as long as it is just running, whereas
the same water would be almost immediately
fatal to a trout or young salmon. The tastiest
gudgeon I ever caught were in a sewer which ran
along the east side of the College meads at
Winchester."

Enjoyable angling may be had with gudgeon,
and the sport is of the most lively kind. Small red-
worms are the best bait, with line well down ; and
if a shoal of fish have once been enticed round
the delicate morsel there is no reason why every
one should not be taken. They fight for the bait,
and the fact of a silvery brother being suddenly
jerked out of his element seems only to whet the
appetite of the next comer. And yet there is considerable skill in gudgeon-fishing. The smaller
fish are apt to toy with the bait, and often manage
to disgorge it more quickly than the angler can
strike after the float disappears. Although gud-

geon may be plentiful enough, they often seem to
be locally distributed in a river, and much of the
success, of course, depends in finding a shoal.
This habit of keeping much together, of being
sequacious, has caused the gudgeon to be named,
in common with roach, the water-sheep, not by any
means on account of supposed stupidity, but from
their follow-my-leader-like movements. In some
parts of the country it is a common practice
before fishing for gudgeon to rake the gravel at
the bottom of the stream or pond. The cloud of
mud as it goes down attracts the fish to its starting-
point in hope of finding food ; and from the fact of
their being able to feed upon such minute
organisms they are rarely disappointed. When a
shoal is once concentrated, the capture of the
individuals is easy. In like spots which the
gudgeon loves best to haunt at ordinary times it
selects for its spawning-ground — among loose
stones and pebbles and shallow water conditions.
The shedding of the spawn takes place in late
April and May, and hatching is soon completed.
By the end of August the fry have attained to an
inch in length, and are able to shift for themselves.
This is one of the easiest fish to keep in confinement, as, with ordinary care, it can be retained in
health for weeks and even months. Fishmongers
keep the fish in vessels until they are required, and

anglers do the same thing when they want fresh bait. In some places gudgeon sell well as an article of food, mostly for invalids, however; and this, as is said, because they are easy of digestion. In appearance this is a pretty little fish, with the upper parts of olive-brown, spotted with black. The irides are orange-red, the lower parts of a silvery white. A light medial line runs along the body, and the tail is faintly barred. Two tiny barbules hang from the angles of the mouth.

IX

CONCERNING SMALL FRY.

I.

ON the fifth day of the dialogue, as reported in *The Complete Angler*, Piscator remarks on the existence of three or four little fish that he had previously forgotten. These were without scales, though they might, for excellency for meat, be compared to any fish of greatest value and largest size. "They breed often," he further remarks, "as it is observed mice and many of the smaller creatures of the earth do ; and as those, so these come quickly to their full growth and perfection. This is needful, for they be, besides other accidents of ruin, both a prey and bait for other fish." All of which statements are true.

Now, if these things are small, they are by no means to be despised ; for there is a tide in the affairs of anglers when these "small fry" of the waters afford as much sport on their pebbly shallows as do the silvery-sided salmon in the pools of Strathspey. For just as Redwings and Fieldfares constitute the first game of young gunners, so the Loach, the Minnow, and the Stickleback are the shiny prey of the youthful angler. We say angler, though as yet he has never handled a rod, save, maybe, such as is constituted by a willow-wand, a bit of string, and a crooked pin. But the average boy has always a considerable dash of the primitive savage in his composition, and this first comes out in relation to fish rather than fowl. See him during his summer holidays as he wantons in the stream like a dace. Watch where his brown legs carry him ; his stealthy movements as he raises the likely stones ; and note that primitive poaching-weapon in his hand. This old pronged fork is every whit as formidable to the loach and bullhead as is the " lister " of the man-poacher to salmon and trout ; and the wader uses it almost as skilfully. He has a bottle on the bank, and into this he pours the fish unhurt which he captures in his hands. Examine his simple aquarium, and hidden among the wet water-weeds you will find three or four species of "small fry." The loach, the minnow, and the bullhead, are sure to be there, with, perhaps, a tiny stickleback ; and somewhere outside the bottle—stuffed in cap or breeches' pocket—crayfish of every age and size.

The little Loach is essentially a fish of the

running-brook and of shallow-water conditions. In haunt and habit it is quite a hermit, and loves to lie under loose, flat stones, from beneath which it is slow to emerge. It is nocturnal in habit, getting quite lively at twilight, and as darkness increases it comes abroad and roams about in search of food. This consists of tiny insects and various kinds of larvæ, and in years gone by we have frequently enticed the "lusty loach" from his dark retreat by dangling before him a small red-worm. This predilection for worms is also seen during a freshet, for then, like trout, the loach gets into the quiet eddies and backwaters waiting for the soft-bodied creatures to pass. Sometimes it may be seen foraging among the aquatic grasses for anything which may have lodged there.

The loach spawns in spring, though the only fact on this head which is known with certainty is its exceeding prolificness. It has been remarked that the loach is particularly active at night, and, when trout-fishing, we have frequently noticed it take to the shallow water, where it seems to enjoy swimming about with its back-fin protruding. Eels feed much upon loach, as do otters, and hence Nature has decreed that the three shall be night-feeders. The body is covered with a smooth, slimy secretion, and it would seem that on this account

many of the water-birds reject them.   In an
extemporised aquarium half-a-dozen loach are
swimming before me.   With the light full upon
them they seem but little inclined to come from
among their sheltering gravel, though now and
again one of them takes a turn round the little
world of waters to see what it can pick up.
These little hermits are pugnacious enough, and
show desperate fight when one offers to invade
the domain of its neighbour.   The most striking
characteristic of the fish are six barbules about
the mouth, which make them resemble barbels
in miniature.   These testify to the fact of their
living at the bottom of streams, and using the
mouth as a sucker in search of food.   These
barbules give the loach its popular name of
"beardie"; it is also known as eelie and
eel-roach.   A close cousin to the loach, and
the only other British fish of the same genera,
is the spined-loach or grounding, a much rarer
species than the foregoing, and less widely distributed.   Like most fishes the loach has the
power to take on itself the colour of the stream
which it haunts, and those before me are greenish
brown, spotted and clouded with darker brown,
and beneath pale, yellowish white.   The irides
are blue ; a medial line runs along the body ; and
the tail is beautifully barred.   Such a delicacy is

the loach to the *gourmet*, that in times past
numbers were, with great trouble, transported
to various European waters; and Frederick, King
of Sweden, had them brought from Germany and
naturalised in his own country.

The Bullhead, or miller's-thumb, must be a
terrible bugbear and goblin to the small fry among
which it lives. He leads a life not unlike that of
the loach, haunting like spots, feeding upon the
same food, and spawning during the first spring
months. A low, flat head, large eyes, wide.
gaping mouth, and body covered with slimy
mucus — these hardly go to form a pleasant
picture. To the juvenile poacher the miller's-
thumb is probably never so popular as the silvery
minnow or the spined stickleback ; but one pe-
culiarity it has over these, and that is its
chameleon-like colours. ' Of a dozen specimens
caught no two are alike. He is yellow, brown,
black, green, creamy ; and doubtless these varying colours are due to the hues of the streams
he inhabits. In summer he indulges himself,
lying on some flat stone for hours, and there
taking his midday *siesta*. The bullhead is even
more formidable to handle than to look at, being
all over protected by spiny armour. The spines are
mostly carried on the fins, and these are frequently
used with considerable effect. The birds of the

waterside often find that they have caught a veritable tartar when they pounce upon the bullhead; and Frank Buckland tells us that he once received a little Grebe (*Podeceps minor*) choked by a miller's-thumb. "The fish," he says, "was so firmly fixed in the bird's mouth that I found it would go neither backwards nor forwards, so I could neither press it down the œsophagus nor pull it out altogether. Mr. Grebe evidently was not aware that the miller's-thumb was armed with two very sharp spikes on each side of the gill-cover, and when the fish found himself in trouble, he simply expanded these spines, which fixed him so firmly in the bird's mouth that it died from suffocation. I have had two or three specimens sent me of Kingfishers destroyed by bullheads sticking in their throats." It is worthy of remark that the presence of spines in a species becomes perfectly well known to the larger predatory fishes, and although trout will take the bullhead dead, eels are the only fish which can manage it alive.

The silvery Minnow is one of the prettiest and most widely distributed of British fresh-water fishes. It belongs to the *Cyprinidæ*, being the tiniest of the fish of the carp kind, and not the least beautiful. "The pink," Walton tells us, "makes a dainty dish of meat," and to make a "minnow-tansy," the little fishes must be fried with yolk of eggs, the flowers of cowslips and of primroses, and a twig of tansy. In colour the minnow is dappled, or waved like a panther, with sky-blue sides, and milk-white belly. "Piscator" sets down "the pink" as a sharp biter, and a fit sporting fish for boys, young anglers, or women that love recreation.

The minnow haunts like spots to those which trout love, and is fond of fresh, running water. Bright, pebbly bottoms it prefers to sediment, and being essentially a social fish, it invariably swims in shoals. If you approach stealthily from the meadow-bank into "Minnow Bay," you may see the pink "at home," and of all little fishes he is the most sprightly and interesting. Watch the silvery shoal in its graceful evolutions, and you will know well what is meant by the poetry of motion. The only fit parallel to a school of silvery minnows in the water, is a flock of burnished starlings in the air. There is no apparent guiding spirit, yet the fifty move like one. They progress as by some hidden force; the water divides before them, and they wave through its liquidness. Minnows have the power common to most fishes of rapidly assimilating to the varying colour of the stream. They change from brown to gold, from gold to brown. To

be seen, the minnow must be sought for; it is
not apparent to the sightless seer. When once
caught, however, it is not difficult to keep in
view, for the tiny green-brown things are ever
active, and the even tenor of their movements
is only at intervals broken by throwing up their
silvery bellies and displaying their bright colours
to the sun. As soon as the minnows eye an
intruder, they move off a foot from the shore,
flicking their tiny dorsal fins the while, and
causing quite a minnow-commotion. When quiet
is restored, they are quick to return, and to watch
them you climb into an overhanging alder bough.

As luck would have it, you have chosen well
your time, and are treated to quite a charming and
unexpected sight ; for another shoal of minnows
has attracted one of the presiding spirits of the
stream. Over there is a stunted, leafless bough,
and a kingfisher has just alighted upon it. At
first his form is motionless ; soon it assumes more
animation ; now is all eye and ear. Then it
darts, hangs for a moment in the air like a kestrel,
and returns to its perch. Again it darts with
unerring aim and secures something. This is
tossed, beaten, and broken with a formidable
beak, and then swallowed head foremost. The
process is again and again repeated, and you find
that the prey is small fish. From watching an

hour, you are entranced at the beauty of the fluttering, quivering thing as the sun shines upon its green and gold vibrations in mid-air. You gain some estimation, too, of the amount of immature fish a pair of kingfishers and their young must destroy in a single season. Later in summer you may see the young brood, with open, quivering wings, and constant calling, as the parent birds fly to and fro. Their plumage is little less brilliant than that of the adult. The hole in which the young are reared is never made by the parent birds, but always by some small burrowing rodent, or occasionally by the little sand-martin. The food of the kingfisher is almost entirely fish—minnows and sticklebacks forming the principal part. Water-beetles, leeches, larvæ, and small trout, as well as the young of coarse fish, are, however, all partaken of at times ; and during the rigour of winter, the kingfishers betake themselves to the estuaries of tidal rivers, where their food of molluscs and shore-haunting creatures is daily replenished. Old naturalists aver that the bird brings up its prey in its feet ; but this is never so, as all food is taken in the beak.

A near view of minnows feeding affords a charming sight. They rummage among the aquatic plants, seize the tiniest morsels of animal

food, and rush after the gauzy-winged ephemeræ.
But a tiny red-worm—what a prize, and what a
commotion it brings! Like a brood of chickens
with an earthworm, every minnow goes pully-haul-
ing away at the delectable morsel as though for
very life. They rush hither and thither, chasing
and chased, fighting and struggling, until their
pink prey is torn into segments, when each rushes
off with what it can get. All this you may watch
in a very modest aquarium; and as the lives of
the little fishes reach out to as much as three years,
there is ample time to form pleasant acquaintance.
This affords opportunity for studying the life-
history of the species, and all its domestic economy
is laid bare to the observer.

Perhaps the period of spawning is the most
interesting, and if you search out a spot where this
is proceeding, this is what you will see : Upon a
bed of clean gravel the female lies with her head
up-stream, and guarded on each side by a smart,
pugnacious gallant. We say smart, for of all the
small fry of the waters, minnows are the most
dandified, and glow with quite a variety of
resplendent colours. Spawning proceeds over
three or four days of early May. Courting trios
are everywhere dotted over the stream. As the
exceedingly small eggs are deposited, they are
impregnated, and show great tenacity in holding

on to where they are thrown down. They attach
themselves to the interstices of the sand and
gravel, and probably hatch in a very few days.
So small are the eggs that they would be difficult
to detect, were it not that they are thrown down
in masses—masses as large as a horse-chestnut.
All the creatures of the waterside assemble at the
minnows' spawning ground; and where possible
the pink ought to be protected. They tend to
keep the water clean and pure, and themselves
afford the most valuable food for salmon and
trout, either in a wild or semi-wild state. Not
only do minnows hatch out rapidly, but grow
rapidly, and by the end of their first summer
they attain to an inch in length. To-day we
scooped up a dozen minnows in our landing-net
from a quiet backwater, and find that they are
done in all the glory of spring colouring. Rose
and purple flash along their sides, and it is this hue
that gives it the pretty, provincial name of pink.

Here is an interesting anecdote anent this
species. In crossing a foot-bridge, a gentleman saw
in the water what he thought to be a flower. Observing it more attentively, it was seen to consist
of a circular assemblage of minnows. Their heads
met in the centre, their tails diverging at equal
distances, and the latter, being elevated above
their heads, gave them the appearance of a flower

G

half-blown. One was longer than the rest; and as often as a straggler came in sight he quitted his post to pursue him, and having driven him away returned to it again, no other minnow offering to take it in his absence. This he repeated several times. The object that attracted them all was a dead minnow, which they seemed to be devouring.

X

CONCERNING SMALL FRY.

II.

QUITE one of the most beautiful of fresh-water
fishes is the Bleak—a pretty little study in green
and silver, and whose technical name implies
"white dace." It rarely attains to any great
size, though it may well be designated a "sporting
fish." Although the angler may hardly think it
worth his while, yet the youthful savages to which
we have referred sometimes test the sporting
qualities of the bleak with considerable success.
Pleasant it is to watch the fish on a summer
evening rushing at every fly that touches the
water. Once, and once only, have we had an
evening with bleak. Staying at a country house,
we discovered that the fish inhabited a large pond
in the orchard, and immediately commenced to
angle for them with the most primitive weapons.
Nevertheless, within a couple of hours we had
done such execution, that we had to desist for

fear of depopulating the pond. The fly used,
be it recorded, was the tiniest artificial black-gnat.

Rather resembling the minnow in general con-
tour, the back of the bleak is iridescent green,
the rest bright silver, with fins white. Add to
this a metallic lustre over all, and it will be seen
that the bleak is a beautiful fish. Whether in
still or running water, bleak are found in shoals,
and being omnivorous feeders they are among
the scavengers of the waters. They take almost
anything that comes down-stream, and are not
unfrequently found at the mouths of sewers.

Considerable interest attaches to bleak from
the fact that artificial pearls are made from their
scales. Fifty years ago the French were great
purchasers of bleak scales from the Thames
fishermen, but now the former supply themselves
from their own rivers. Besides the enormous
quantity of these pearls used in France, the value
of their export is over one million francs. " The
art of making imitation pearls is ascribed to
one Jacquin, a chaplet and rosary manufacturer,
at Passey, 1680. Noticing the water after
cleaning some white fish (*Leuciscus alburnus*),
a species of dace, he gradually collected the
sediment, and with this substance (to which he
gave the name of *essence d'orient*) and with a
thin glue made of parchment, he lined the glass

beads, and afterwards filled them with wax. The method of making the round bead is by heating one end of a glass tube and blowing into it two or three times, which then expands into a globular form. The workman then separates the bead, places the end which has been heated on a wire, and heats the other end. This process is called bordering or edging. The best pearls are made in the same way, the holes of the tubes being gradually reduced by heat to the size of those of the real pearls, the workman taking each bead on an inserted wire, and, by continually turning them round in the flame of the lamp used, they become so true as to be strung as evenly as the Oriental pearls. The lamp used is similar to a glass-blower's foot-bellows apparatus, and the work is done by lamplight, daylight being unsuitable. Seven pounds' weight of fish-scales give one pound of *essence d'orient.*"—*Land and Water.*

Eels are among the mysteries of creation, and this is the more puzzling as they are the most common and widely distributed of fishes. Less is known concerning them than almost any other of our British fresh-water species. The eel is just such a creature as would centre about it superstition; and in many country districts it is not considered a fish at all, but a " water-serpent." The mighty conger is cousin to the eels proper, the "sharp" and "broad" nosed varieties respectively. We have already had occasion to remark on the colours of fishes—their beauty, their variety, and, above all, the inherent power possessed by most of rapidly changing from one colour to another. In every case this is probably done for protective reasons, and no fish is such an adept at colour-transformation as the eel. There is every shade of colour, from silvery white to golden brown, and black; and it is noticed that these hues have direct relation to the haunt in which the fish happen to be.

One of the great characteristics of eels is what is called their "eel-fare"—the passage of "elvers." This passage is a most remarkable part in the fish's economy, though it can hardly be said to be constant. In some rivers it takes place in spring, in others in summer, and always in enormous numbers. The eels that take passage up the rivers are about three inches in length, and it has been computed that nearly twenty thousand passed a given point in the space of a minute. Nearly all eels are nocturnal in their habits, though these tiny elvers travel only by day, resting during the night. Their movements vary in different rivers. Where the bed of the stream is rocky, and its current swift, they form themselves into a closely-compacted body,

as though to aid their progress; though where
the water is logged or shallow, each fish moves
at its individual pleasure.   A host of aquatic
creatures follow the " eel-fare " and feed upon
its members.   Herons, kingfishers, coots, water-
hens, and grebes may be found in its wake, filling
themselves to repletion on its tiny members.
There are other enemies beside these, for many
obstacles bar the course, and at this time elvers
suffer great mortality.   It has been truly remarked
that the passing up a river of the young eels is
one of the most curious sights in natural history;
and the perseverance of these little creatures in
overcoming all obstructions they may encounter
is quite extraordinary.   The large flood-gates,
sometimes fifteen feet in height, to be met with on
the Thames, might be supposed sufficient to bar
the progress of a fish the size of a darning-
needle.   But young eels have a wholesome idea
that nothing can stop them; consequently nothing
does.   As one writer says, speaking of the way
in which they ascend flood-gates and such-like
barriers :—" Those which die stick to the post;
others, which get a little higher, meet with the
same fate, until at last a sufficient layer of them
is formed to enable the rest to overcome the
difficulty of the passage.   The mortality resulting
from such ' forlorn hopes ' greatly helps to ac-

count for the difference in number of young eels
on their upward migration, and of those which
return down - stream in the autumn. In some
places these baby eels are much sought after, and
are formed into cakes, which are eaten fried."

Eels spawn like other fishes, though for a long
period the most remarkable theories were held
as to their birth. One of the old beliefs was that
they sprang from mud ; and a rival theory held
that young eels developed from fragments sepa-
rated from their parents' bodies by rubbing against
rocks. One old author not only declared that
they came from May-dew, but gave the following receipt for producing them : " Cut up two
turfs covered with May-dew, and lay them one
upon the other, the grassy sides inwards, and
then expose them to the heat of the sun ; in a
few hours there will spring from them an infinite
quantity of eels."

Four, or at most five species of Stickleback are
known to British naturalists. These are distin-
guished according to the number of spines which
they carry, and those mentioned above have
three, four, five, ten, and fifteen respectively. All
the sticklebacks are tiny fishes, though owing to
several characteristics they are remarkably interesting. They have a marvellous power of conforming
to any and every environment, and are found in

pond and ditch, fresh water and salt—even in brackish estuaries.

When any common object has a great many provincial names, be assured that it is dear to dwellers in the country. A general favourite, the stickleback has upwards of thirty *aliases*, and this is probably owing to the fact of its being a nest-builder. As in the case of a considerable number of animals and birds, fish assume brighter and more glowing colours as the breeding season advances. And this is particularly true of the stickleback at the time of nest-building. Now his colours become bright and intense; his under-parts glow with silvery crimson, and his eyes and cheeks are metallic lustred. With the light full upon him he is almost transparent, and now he assumes a warlike disposition.

The following, however, shows the whole breeding economy of the stickleback as observed by the Curator of the Norwich Museum :—" Two glass troughs filled with aquatic plants and animals were provided, into which a solitary individual of either species was inducted. Each made himself quite at ease ; and a female companion being introduced into the domicile, he was not long in commencing the work of nidification. The appearance of the three-spined stickleback was exceedingly beautiful. The little creature's throat and belly were of

a bright-red colour, and his eyes of a brilliant
bluish-green, having a perfectly metallic lustre,
not unlike the green feathers of a humming-bird ;
the whole fish seemed somewhat translucent,
and glowing with an internal brightness. He
selected a spot nearly in the centre of the trough,
and busily set to work to make a collection of
delicate fibrous materials, resting on the ground,
and matted into an irregular circular mass, somewhat depressed, and upwards of an inch in diameter,
the top being covered with similar materials, and
having in the centre a rather large hole. His
work was commenced at noonday, and was completed and the eggs deposited by half-past six in the
afternoon. Nothing could exceed the attention
from this time evinced by the male fish. He kept
constant watch over the nest, every now and then
shaking up the materials and dragging out the
eggs, and then pushing them into their receptacle again, and tucking them up with his snout,
arranging the whole to his mind, and again and
again adjusting it until he was satisfied ; after
which, he hung or hovered over the surface of
the nest, his head close to the orifice, the body
inclined upwards at an angle of about forty-five
degrees, fanning it with the pectoral fins, aided by
a side motion of the tail. This curious manœuvre
was apparently for the purpose of ventilating the

spawn ; at least by these means a current of water
was made to set in towards the nest, as was
evident by the agitation of particles of matter
attached to it. This fanning, or ventilation, was
frequently repeated every day until the young
were hatched, and sometimes the little fellow
would dive head foremost into his nursery and
bring out a mouthful of sand, which he would
carry to some distance and discharge with a puff.
At the end of a month, the young ones were
first perceived. The nest was built on the 23rd
of April, the young appeared first on May 21st.
Unremitting as had been the attention of this
exemplary parent up to the time of the hatching
of the eggs, he now redoubled his assiduity. He
never left the spot either by night or by day,
and during the daytime he guarded it most pertina-
ciously, allowing nothing to approach. If any of
the water animals chanced to come near, he would
instantly pounce upon them, and unceremoniously
shove or tumble them over. If a stick or quill
were passed down from the top of the vessel, he
struck it fiercely, and with such smartness that
the blow was distinctly felt by the hand. The
fry were at first so minute and transparent
that they were scarcely perceptible, and it was
only by a slight fluttering motion their position
could be occasionally discovered, otherwise it was

impossible to detect them. They were for a time confined to the meshes of the nest and its near neighbourhood, but by degrees were allowed greater space, and the parent fish hollowed out a sort of small basin for them, in which they disported themselves until they were strong enough to take a wider range. In consequence of there being no other fish in the vessel, we did not see the battles and stratagems which are carried on between companion and rival fishes when engaged in similar parental duties. The encounters upon such occasions are said to be fearful and prolonged, and it is not without reason the young nestlings are so carefully guarded, as acts of cannibalism are not infrequent."

ONCE SILVER STREAMS.

THERE is, and always has been, something fascinating about running water. Savages name their
children after it, and their songs and legends
are full of allusions to it. Not only is this
so with primitive people, but enlightened ones.
Even now, men direct their roads by the waterways, and for reasons far other than those of
trade and commerce. What these reasons are
may be known to every walker by the waterside
if only he possesses eyes, and knows how to
use them. No one knew better than Charles
Kingsley what charms there are about brightly-
running streams, and none enjoyed them more
than he. And this because he was an angler.
He knew and said that he saw a hundred sights,
and heard a hundred sounds, that were hidden
from the traveller on the dusty highway. The
pedestrian of the road sees only the outside of
the land—sees only its commonplace sights; but
the angler is brought face to face with Nature's

secrets—the flowers, and birds, and insect-life of
the rich river-banks. Here man never interferes;
here everything is wild—wood and water, where
everything flourishes, and the drought never comes.
Rivers and streams are the chief arteries of the land,
and yield to a host of field and woodland creatures
the life-giving elements. The waters themselves
teem with myriad life, and that of a higher
organisation is everywhere along the banks.

That the running brooks and still waters of
this country still contain plenty of fish for the
naturalist to base his experiments upon there can
be no question; but as to how far these afford
food for the people is a quite different matter.
Those who know practically about the cultivation
of fresh-water fishes, either in a wild or semi-
wild state, know how much yet remains to be
done—how there exists the terrible subject of
pollution, upon which the law has but feebly laid
its hand. The foulest pollution is yet carried
on with impunity; and it would seem that, in
spite of much half legislation, there is no power
in the land to stop it. And what is the outcome
of this? The fresh, bright streams have become
in many places the swift scavengers of all that
is foul and filthy. The once silvery foam of
their waterfalls now comes down black as ink;
life has gone from them, the flowers and trees

have disappeared from their banks. Many of the best-known rivers and streams have been depopulated of their pink-spotted denizens, and have become such that no pure thing can live in them. Were there any shingly beaches, or any pebble beds, spawn would never hatch upon them ; or were this possible, nothing hatched could long survive.

Even now, pollution has done its worst. Within the past dozen years, many salmon and trout rivers have been depopulated to an alarming extent, and the causes that have contributed to this end are on the increase. The late Richard Jefferies, in one of his charming essays, says : "It is the birds and other creatures peculiar to the water that render fly-fishing so pleasant ; were they all destroyed, and nothing left but the mere fish, one might as well stand and angle in a stone cattle-trough." But then the fish are gone, too. And this being so, it may be well to take one river as the type of many, and see what phases of life have gone from it. Once it was a famous trout-stream, and men who wrote books on angling—the kings of their craft —came to kill trout in its waters. But now there are none to kill. A dozen mills pour their dye-washes and waste into the stream, covering its pebbly bottom with a filthy sediment, so

destroying every natural "redd." There is never
a spawning ground along miles of its reaches,
and the poacher has given up his trade. Even
among the jute fibres from the paper-mills, the
scourings from the woollen-mills, the fish manage
for a time to drag out a precarious existence.
Then the fine mechanism of the gill becomes
coated, and the fish sickens and dies—is suffocated, in fact. As the salmon and trout are
weakened, they gradually lose power to work
against the force of the current, and are washed
far down - stream. Hence it is that the dead
fish are never found near the source of pollution, and the blame is invariably cast upon the
wrong person. The kind of pollution indicated
is mostly done by private proprietors; but even
worse offenders are Corporate bodies, who in
most cases are the only competent authorities
to set the preventive legal machinery at work
to stem the evil. It is often urged that to obtain
the purity of the rivers, a host of manufactures
would have to be curtailed. But this is by no
means necessarily so. Much of the pollution of
to-day is owing simply to the selfishness of the
pollutor. Appliances there are in plenty which
would save the river and only lightly touch the
manufacturer's pocket. But why should he go
to any expense when the Local Authority connives

at his transgression by helping to turn the river
into a vast open sewer? So long as the "Authority"
pours filthy excrement into the river, the local
manufacturer has them on the hip, and is safe.
This Sanitary Authority for the most part consists of magistrates and manufacturers; of men
whose interests are so identical that they tacitly
agree that the townsfolk may play the part of
the shuttlecock to their battledores. And all
this in spite of the fact that these same townsfolk have paid, by their hardly-got earnings, a
hundred thousand pounds for the carrying out
of a main-sewage scheme, in order that the purity
of the river might be for ever retained.

Then there are those thousand objects of the
river-side, which have such a healthful influence
upon the inhabitants. Many of the trees stand
starkly outlined against the sky, with great black
skeleton limbs, the hoisted "black flags" of Nature,
proclaiming each that a life has been sacrificed
—to pollution. The birds and flowers have gone,
and we have in their place a vast line of inky
desolation, unrelieved by colour or life. What
impresses one most is the desolation, and silence,
and bare coldness that seem to have taken
possession of the lifeless stream. Where are
the moorhens that rustled among the reeds; the
kingfisher in green and gold; the white-breasted

dipper on the mossy stones, the coots, the grebes, the teal, the blue heron of the shallows? All are gone—a sacrifice to pollution. Once there were salmon and trout, pike, perch, roach, and bream; these have gone the way of the birds. Once the otter haunted the quiet pools, but it left them when its food ceased. Once there were water-rats, voles, shrews, and mice; these were long ago thinned out of existence. There were the gauzy-winged flies, too, so exquisite of form and colour, that were characteristic of the anglers' months—from dry March to sodden October; the trout-loved denizens of the streams, the ephemeræ. But these vanished at the very first sign of pollution. And now that all these are gone, our typical rivulet is what it is, a foul, unlovely stream, destitute of life. Pollution is indirectly responsible, too, for the disease which periodically affects the fish in the rivers and lakes of this country. Some few years ago this scourge played terrible havoc in many of the best northern streams, especially those which were systematically polluted. Whether it is true that pollution is the first cause of disease may be open to question; but it is certain that fish once so afflicted never recover, save in water of the purest description.

To look at the question of pollution, however, merely from Nature's standpoint may be too narrow; there is the far more important question of Sanitation. And this applies to our larger fresh-water lakes as well as to rivers. A short time ago it was said that Windermere was neither more nor less than a gigantic cesspool. This was an exaggerated statement; but there was probably much truth in it. Others of the lakes are almost in worse plight. Ulleswater is the receptacle of much foreign matter, which is as injurious to health as to fish life, and certain species have almost been driven from those parts nearest the lead-mines. In short, there is no northern lake which is absolutely pure. The sacrifice to pollution, then, is so great and so widespread as to be almost beyond belief, and in a few years it will have caused such devastation as can never be remedied. Fish life may be returned to its natural haunts if once legislation would stop pollution. But there seems very little inclination to do this, nor will there be until the country is thoroughly awakened to what is going on, and to an appreciation of that of which it is being deprived.

XII

FISH STEWS.

ARCHÆOLOGICAL investigations in the north are constantly bringing to light remains of two institutions which once played a not unimportant part in the domestic economy of our ancestors. These are Pigeon Cotes and Fish Stews. They were mostly attached to the old manor-houses and baronial halls, and probably at one time there were few of these strongholds without them. To fully appreciate the value of their products, we must go back to a time when the art of fattening cattle was but little understood and rarely practised. At this period the supply of animal food proved wholly inadequate to the demands of the community, for the stock fed out of doors in autumn was killed off by Christmas, and but little fresh meat, except veal, appeared in the markets before the ensuing midsummer. The more substantial yeomen and manufacturers provided against this inconvenience by curing a quantity of beef at Martinmas, the greatest part of which they pickled in brine, the rest being dried and smoked by being hung in the chimney. Hogs were slaughtered after Christmas, the flesh being principally converted into bacon ; and this, with the dried beef and dried mutton, afforded a change of salt meat in the spring. The fresh provisions of winter consisted of eggs, poultry, geese, and ill-fed veal, calves being conveyed to market when only a fortnight old.

These things constituted the food of the upper middle-class of the country districts, and it was only those still higher who could draw upon the " Culver-house " and the Fish-stew. To them fresh fish and plump pigeons were always at hand to furnish a pleasant change from the hard salted meat. At this time the old British pastime of falconry had not yet gone out, and duck, heron, and moorfowl were often found at table. In the wilder parts of the north, red-deer, fallow, or roe still held the older woods of the hills, and venison in season was always welcome. Every religious house had its fish stew, as had the old halls, and both monks and barons kept their " noble and deynteous fyssche " for fast days, feasts, and general use.

> Full many a fair partrich hadde they in mewe,
> And many a breme and many a luce in stewe.

The " partrich " was, of course, the partridge,
though it was much easier and more profitable to
keep domestic pigeons in store than wild game-
birds in pound. There were good reasons—other
than those of luxury and comfort—for setting such
store by the delicacies of fresh fish and flesh.
The prevalent diet has been referred to, and
there is no wonder that anything that could vary
or palliate it was eagerly cultivated. But there
was another reason. Those who were too poor
to afford salt meat subsisted upon rye-bread and
fish, and what with the indigestible food of the
rich, and the too meagre diet of the poor,
ague was of terrible frequency, and leprosy common. These must be ascribed to the unwhole-
some food and privations of the people, for both
disappeared as esculent vegetables came to be
cultivated, and salted provisions fell in repute.

Macaulay reminds us of the fish-ponds in
which carp and tench were fattened for the table ;
the warrens of conies, and the large round dove-
cot rising in the immediate neighbourhood of the
abodes of the great and wealthy, of the castle, the
convent, and the manor-house. To-day there
is hardly an old hall or religious house in
the country which does not show traces of
its fish stew, or where this is wanting, the name
is almost certain to belong to some part of

the demesne, showing where it formerly stood. The monks knew a great deal about the cultivation of ponds, the breeding and rearing of fish, and their subsequent management and fattening in the stews. This art is still much practised in certain European countries, where the conditions to-day are like those which prevailed in England two or three centuries ago. Most of the fish fatted were used upon fast days. In close connection with this is the fact that the ruins of almost every monastery in the country has its stew, and such manor-houses as were occupied by Catholic families. As well as introducing many rare and dainteous fish from the Continent, the monks reduced the cultivation of fish-ponds to a science. It was customary to have a series of these, which grew in turn both fish and vegetables. The ponds were so arranged that they could be drained at will; and periodically the water was run from the first, the fish being caught as it emptied, and transported to the second. No. 1 was then planted with oats, barley, or rye grass, the crop being reaped as it matured; and as winter came round it was re-stocked with fry and yearlings. By this process it was not only sweetened, but its supply of food was greatly improved, with the result that the fish turned into it grew and fattened in an extraordinary manner.

When each of the ponds had been worked in
rotation, one was growing a crop of vegetables,
another fry and yearlings, and the third breeders,
and fish fattening for the market. Suitable
weeds were grown about the margins of the
ponds, and in many instances much care was
taken in the matter of feeding. As the fish grew
to a large size they were netted and placed in
the actual stew. An ingenious contrivance for
taking these out at pleasure was a strong wooden
box, having holes in the bottom, which was
sunk where the water was deepest. As required,
the box was wound up with a chain, contents
and all.

A great variety of fish were kept in the ponds,
and fatted in the stews when these were in vogue.
Among them were carp, tench, pike, eels, trout,
and many others. Thought was given to the
habits of these, and while tench and eels succeeded best in mud, carp were kept on gravelly
bottoms. Certain fish devoured the spawn of
others, and care had to be taken to protect one
species against its neighbours. On this account,
carp and tench thrive and breed best when no
other fish are put with them into the same pond.
Walton reminds us that in stocking a pond with
carp, it is necessary to put into it two or three
milters for one spawner, and that it should have

certain characteristics. It should be stony or
sandy, warm and free from wind, not deep, and
have willows and grass on its sides. Then he
notes that carp usually breed in marl-pits, or such
as have clean clay bottoms, and are new. The
pike, or "luce," as it was called, was in great
request for fattening in stews, as it grew with
great rapidity. The char, one of the most beautiful and dainty of British fishes, is said to have
been introduced by the monks, as doubtless were
the various species of carp. Carp-culture on the
Continent is quite an important industry, and in
ancient days this fish was in great repute for the
table. Of late much attention has been paid to
its cultivation ; but in the "*Boke of St. Albans*"
it is described as "a deigntous fysshe, but scarce."
It is little wonder that the monks were alive to
the merits of carp, for no fish was better adapted
to thrive in the stews and fish-ponds, where the
monks usually kept their finny live stock. In both
France and Germany carp - culture is quite an
important industry, and a great many persons are
engaged in it, both men and women. The tench
being a fish of contented mind, almost any kind
of conditions will suit his temperament. As a
store fish he is invaluable, and in any case gives
nearly no trouble. Of all the fish of pond or
stew, the tench is the most accommodating.

Like the carp, he can be conveyed long distances to market, and, if not sold, can be brought back to await another occasion for sale. Bream, as a stew fish, has been appreciated since the time of Chaucer ; and Walton, in his admiration, refers to him as "large and stately." Bream, like tench, are fond of still, quiet waters, with soft soil bottoms, and in which they find their chief sustenance. The fish has been known to attain to 17 pounds in weight, though this of course is exceptional. There is a French proverb to the effect that " He that hath breams in his pond is able to bid his friend welcome"; and if the bream is toothsome, he is equally good as a sporting fish.

These are some of the fresh-water fish which once occupied the stews in this country, and might with profit do so again.

XIII

THE DEPOPULATION AND RE-STOCKING OF TROUT-STREAMS.

DURING the past twenty years the trout-streams of this country have been depopulated to the extent of from fifty to a hundred per cent. The more fortunate rivers are in the former case; whilst many famous trout-streams that once were, have become too poisonous for fish to live in at all.

The causes which have contributed to this state of things are few, but are alarmingly on the increase. Chief among them is pollution by town sewage and mill refuse; and those who, in the first case, are alone competent to set the legal machinery at work are usually the greatest offenders. These are the Corporations of towns. In a case of summary proceedings for pollution* the prosecution must prove "dead fish." But direct proof of this kind is often unobtainable.

* Under 24 & 25 Vict., Cap. 109, Sec. 5.

No member of the migratory or non-migratory *Salmonidæ* will spawn either upon mud or sediment. But, unfortunately, they do this sometimes ere the deposit is thrown down. Then what ensues? Protect the stream as you will from heron, duck, and waterfowl, and from 1,000,000 eggs with which the stream is spawned, not more than a very small percentage of fry will come forth. The spawning-beds of rivers must be pure and clean, else no successful hatching can take place. Where solid matter is held in suspension over a spawning-bed the eggs are suffocated, and any few that may escape usually turn out to be deformed fish. This is owing to the clogging of the outer wall of the cell-sac, which interferes with the equal absorption of oxygen from the water. Therefore, where this sort of pollution exists, the absolute extinction of trout is certain at no very distant date.

Of late years disease has played terrible havoc in some of the best northern streams. In one river I could name, scarcely a fish can be caught which does not show in some way marks left by disease—want of tail, partial loss of fins, white patches on the skin, where the fungus has previously grown. That numbers of the fish attacked do survive there can be no question; and that the disease may be prevented at the cost of a few fish I have but little doubt. In these days of artificial rearing, restocking, and preservation generally, anglers and angling associations are apt either to forget or to ignore the balance of Nature. They destroy her appointed agents, and then fail to understand her consistent revenge. Now Nature rarely overlooks an insult. That the pink-spotted trout may live, a whole host of stream-haunting creatures are condemned; and this, too, often on the most insufficient evidence. Numerous waterfowl—the coot, rail, kingfisher, dipper—are said to be injurious to the interests of anglers, because they destroy the ova on the " redds." But it is doubtful whether there is any serious foundation for the charge, except in the case of the kingfisher; and Frank Buckland it was who said that one might as well shoot a swallow skimming over a turnip-field, as a dipper over the spawning-beds in autumn. Even the harmless water-vole, which is a vegetarian, and feeds upon the thick, succulent stalks of aquatic plants, has been denounced as a destroyer of spawn. But the creature against which the orthodox angler " breathes hot roarings out " is the Otter. Yet how few fish does the Otter really destroy! The evidence to be gathered by those who live along its streams all goes to show that fresh-water crayfish form the staple of its food. It wanders miles in a night in search of this dainty, and will not partake of soft-bodied fish so long as this crustacean can be found. But the economy of the otter ought not to be overlooked in connection with our fish supply. Probably its increasing rarity has as much to do with disease as had the extermination of the nobler birds of prey with the grouse disease. A falcon always takes the easiest flight at its prey;[*] the otter, when fishing, captures the slowest fish. In each case they kill off the weakest, the most diseased, and thereby secure the survival of the fittest. Corporations are to blame in another particular. In seeking to prevent floods, all obstacles—natural boulders, rocks, and the trunks of trees—are removed from the river bed. This takes away the harbours of the fish without succeeding in its object; for the old and disused weirs that exist on many trout-streams are important factors in preventing the rapid flow of water. Another thing to be considered is the nature of the dressings put on land in the shape of manure. The soluble parts, often poisonous, are carried by the rains into the stream; and, nowadays, drainage is rapid —much more so than formerly, when streams took days to rise and fall. This brought food; but now surface-water is quickly directed into channels, and as quickly conveyed into the river.

---

[*] This has been denied from an authoritative quarter, but I prefer to let the statement stand.

Depopulation naturally leads to the important subject of restocking. We have in England hundreds of thousands of acres of fallow water, waiting only for the application of labour and knowledge to yield tons of fish food annually. This applies not so much to rivers as to the larger fresh-water areas, such as are found, for instance, in the English Lake District. Here the lakes are isolated, and all those conflicting interests are cut out which usually are present where sea-going *Salmonidæ* are placed in rivers. In the district indicated, the benefits would be directly reaped by those upon whom the original cost of restocking devolved. The Lake District, or other Fishery Boards, might undertake the experiment. But what more nearly concerns us now is the restocking of such rivers and streams as have been depopulated. Streams, as a rule, afford more sport than food supply; but it is difficult to draw the line between these and the great salmon- and trout-producing rivers. Tributaries are the great natural "redds" or spawning-grounds, not only of rivers, but of lakes and sea-lochs. It matters not whether restocking takes place by ova, fry, yearlings, or two-year-old fish — these are invariably turned into tributary streams a mile or so above their outlets.

The artificial hatching and rearing of fresh-water fish is inexpensive and easy under anything like favourable conditions. The larger and more wealthy fishing associations adopt this method of stocking or restocking their waters; a method which has the great advantage that fish can be hatched in very great numbers, suitable to large areas. The process of hatching is long, and we cannot here speak of it. The eggs hatch into avelins, which, as soon as they begin to feed, are termed fry. The nutrition of the avelin is gained from the yolk-sac, which still attaches to it. Prior to the total absorption of this the immature fish are stationary, and do not absorb oxygen—or to such a small extent that they cannot die of oxygen starvation. If turned down into streams with pebbly shallows, they sink into the sheltering gravel; and when the process of absorption is completed, they begin life as fry. The characteristics of the avelin, which we have pointed out, make it easy and safe of transport.

Fry and yearling fish are most used for the purposes of restocking. The former are lively little things, about an inch long, and if turned out under anything like favourable conditions soon begin to fare for themselves. If fairly acclimatised, they may be turned into the streams after they have been feeding for about a couple of months. In doing this they should be handled as little as possible. They are easily injured, easily killed; and it is somewhat remarkable that an injury, apparently slight, produces disease, one of the symptoms of which is a whitish fungoid growth that is, perhaps, infectious. Whenever fry are transferred they should be poured from tank to tank, and even, if practicable, into the stream; every sort of net for transferring should be discarded. As a commercial commodity these fish are exceedingly inexpensive. Robust fish that have been feeding a month may be obtained at as low a rate as two pounds per thousand, and even less if great quantities are purchased. In the case of fresh-water lakes, sea-lochs, or rivers in which large fish already exist, it is always advisable to turn in fry a mile or so above the outlet, whence they will descend in from eight to eighteen months. One of the great secrets of success in turning down fry is that the streams in which they are to begin the battle of life are suitable to their requirements. The stream, in the first place, must be absolutely without pollution; it must have a clean gravel bed, with many little bays and eddies. The young fish love to haunt the bright, pebbly reaches, as these afford them the greatest protection. The more thickly grown the banks are with plants and trees, and

the stream-margin with brambles and cresses,
the better. The first bring food, the second
afford protection. About four inches of running
water is probably the ideal depth for fry. They
may be "sown" in the stream as local conditions
suggest. The sowing ought always to be done
proceeding down-stream; "hides" and "rests" for
the fish should be inserted. These are com-
posed of two bits of brick placed about four
inches apart, and covered in with a piece of
slate. Into these the fry dart, and are safe
from their larger enemies, of which they have
many. One great advantage of turning fry
into brooks is that in time of "freshets" and
floods they are enabled to get into the quiet
eddies, and are not swept down by the rushing
waters.

When the fish of which we have been speaking descend from the streams, they are from
two to four inches in length, and are known as
"yearlings." These are turned down in the
spring months, and from their age and size, a
greater percentage survive than in the case of fry.
As the fish increase in size, they have fewer, but
larger enemies. Otters, probably, do little harm
to trout at this stage of their growth, preferring,
as they pass up the shallow streams in summer,
other game. Fry are often kept to grow into

yearlings in boxes, or "nurseries." It is pleasant then to watch the progress they make, to see how tame they become, and the manner in which they rush out and wait about at feeding time. Every angler has watched how the smaller wild trout act in early summer, when the myriads of black gnats revolve just over the water. In the nurseries the little fish act in precisely the same way, jump and throw themselves out of the water, and gambol in the most frolicsome fashion.

It is almost useless to turn down small fish in large sheets of water where great numbers of predatory fishes, such as pike, already exist. This applies with greater force where there are few shallow-water conditions, which means that small fish have absolutely no means of escape. Probably the most effectual method of stocking such water—deep fresh-water lakes, reservoirs, etc. —is by two-year-old trout, or even older. Fish at this age have attained to six or eight inches, and, if turned out in early spring, often make upwards of half a pound by the end of the ensuing summer. These two-year-olds can be purchased at £25 a thousand, whilst yearlings may be bought at less than half that price; and in either case, with skilful care, there is little risk in transit. Of course, larger fish than these can be obtained for money—trout from two to five pounds in weight—which will give immediate sport. But as the *Salmonidæ* increase in size the difficulty of carriage greatly increases, and even if safely turned out, they want time to get used to the natural *ephemeræ*, in place of the artificial food of the commercial fishery.

XIV.

WATER POACHERS.

In November, both salmon and trout are making
up-stream in considerable numbers, seeking out
the "redds," which will constitute their spawning-
grounds. Although the enemies of salmon, trout,
and char are numerous and ever-present, the fish
suffer most when they are lying on the spawning-
beds in a semi-torpid condition. On the upper
reaches of trout-streams hundreds of fish are now
spawning, lying side by side on the clean gravel
in such numbers as to constitute shoals. This
crowding on the "redds" proves injurious to
the fish, as the fungoid growth, which is so
terrible a disease, is transferred from one to
another; if, indeed, this crowding is not the
original cause of disease. In the case of salmon
and trout, estimates vary as to the number of
fish that reach maturity; this being variously
estimated at one from every 1,000 to 6,000 eggs
deposited.

The first and great destruction takes place on the
"redds." Everywhere over these are tiny raised
heaps of gravel, sheltering the spawn. But the
shelter is insufficient to guard it from devouring
enemies. These are in the air, on the land,
in the water. Many members of the hungry
Salmonidæ themselves prey on the spawn, and it
is difficult to cope with them. Bunches of wild
duck and teal seek out the "redds" in autumn,
and feed on right through the night unless dis-
turbed. Thither, too, as I have daily witnessed,
the swan leads her cygnets; and it is known that
one of these large birds will destroy nearly a
gallon of ova in a day. "My swan and her crew"
would have disposed of 2,400,000 eggs in that
time. I know now of more than one northern
trout-stream which has been totally depopulated
of fish simply by the large number of water-fowl
kept upon them. There are many fish that never
spawn, and these, together with the growing
yearlings, are always on the look-out for eggs
over the reaches. Sometimes the parent itself
will destroy the spawn. Secreted among the
thick herbage of the river-bank, I have been at
pains to find out which were the worst enemies
of the *Salmonidæ*, and, to make these observations
the more accurate, I have shot and afterwards
carefully examined the creatures that haunt the

ponds at Stormontfield, where, upon a heron being shot, it disgorged more than fifty fry.

One of the most curious enemies of British fresh-water fishes is a small floating water-weed—the Bladderwort. Along its branches are a number of small green vesicles or bladders, which, being furnished with tiny jaws, seize upon the tiny fishes, which are assimilated into its substance. This is a subtle poacher, the true character of which has only lately been detected.

When salmon and trout are upon the spawning-beds their senses seem to become dulled, and they are more easily approached than at other times. Although the otter is usually regarded as an enemy, it may be that he plays a beneficial part in the economy of nature. He certainly destroys fewer fish than is generally supposed ; and his presence near the spawning-beds in some rivers is, to my certain knowledge, indirectly beneficial to pisciculturists. He kills off the slowest, weakest, and diseased fish, and therefore helps to eradicate disease.

The man poacher gets a large share of the spawning fish. He obtains these in various ways —according to the approved local method. The salmon offers a fair mark, and he spears it ; whilst trout are taken in nets in enormous quantities. But fish food taken in this way is insipid and

tasteless.   Yet it is eaten in poor rural neighbour-
hoods ; the fish costing only about twopence a
pound.   Guns are sometimes used to secure big
fish, as are "click" hooks.   Both these methods
require lights, which the poacher secures in the
shape of burning tar-brands.   All through the
close season there is constant watching and war
between the poachers and the water-bailiffs ; but,
despite the exertions of the latter, cartloads of
salmon are often taken from the "redds" in a
single night.

XV

THE FISH-POACHER.

FISH-POACHING is practised none the less for the high preservation and stricter watching which is so characteristic of the times. In outlying country towns, with salmon- and trout-streams in the vicinity, it is carried on to an almost incredible extent. There are many men who live by it, and women to whom it constitutes a thriving trade. These know neither times nor seasons, and, like the heron and the kingfisher, poach the whole year round. They provide the chief business of the country police-court, and the great source of profit to the local fish and game dealer. The wary poacher never starts for his fishing-grounds without having first his customer; and it is surprising with what lax code of morals the provincial public will deal when the silent night worker is one to the bargain. Of course, the public always gets cheap fish and fresh fish—so fresh, indeed, that the life has not yet gone out of it.

It is a perfectly easy matter to poach fish, but the difficulty lies in conveying them into the towns and villages. The poacher never knows but that he may meet some county constable along the unfrequented country roads, and consequently never carries his game with him. This he secretes in stacks, and ricks, and disused farm buildings, until such times as they may be safely sent for. Country carriers, early morning milk-carts, and women are all employed in getting the fish into town. In this the women are most successful. Sometimes they may be seen labouring under a heavy load carried in a sack, with faggots and rotten sticks protruding from the mouth; or, again, with a large basket innocently covered with crisp green cresses, which effectually hide the bright, silvery fish beneath.

The methods of the fish-poacher are many. The chances of success, too, are greatly in his favour, for he works silently and always in the night. He walks abroad much during the day, and makes mental notes of men and fish. He knows the beats of the watchers, and has the waterside, as it were, by heart. He can work in the dark as well as in the light, and this is essential to his silent trade.

During summer and when the water becomes low, the fish congregate in deep "dubs." This they do for protection, and if overhung with trees there is here always abundance of food. If a poacher intends to net a "dub," he carefully examines every inch of its bottom beforehand. If it has been thorned, he carefully removes these—small thorn-bushes with stones attached, thrown in by the watchers to entangle the poachers' nets, and so allow the fish to escape. At night the poacher comes, unrolls his long net on the pebbles, and then commences operations at the bottom of the river reach. The net is dragged by a man at each side, a third wading after to lift it over the stakes, and so prevent the fish from escaping. When the end of the pool is reached, the trout are simply drawn out upon the pebbles. This is repeated through the night until half-a-dozen pools are netted, and, maybe, depopulated of their fish.

Netting of this description is a wholesale method of destruction, always supposing that the poachers are allowed their own time. It requires to be done slowly, however, and, if alarmed, they can do nothing but abandon their net and run. This is necessarily large, and when thoroughly wet is a most cumbersome thing and exceedingly heavy. The capturing of a net stops the depredations of the poachers for a while, as these, being large, take long to knit. For narrower streams, pretty much the same method as that indicated above is used, only the net is smaller, and to it are attached two poles. The method of working this is precisely similar to that of the last.

A species of poaching, which the older hands rarely go in for, is that of poisoning. Chloride of lime is the agent most in use, as it does not injure the edible parts. This is thrown into the river where fish are known to lie, and its deadly influence is soon seen. The fish become poisoned and weakened, and soon float belly uppermost. This at once renders them conspicuous, and, as they are on the surface of the stream, they are simply lifted out of the water with a landing-net. This is a most wholesale and cowardly method, as it frequently poisons the fish for miles down-stream; it not only kills the larger fish, but destroys great quantities of immature ones, which are wholly unfit for food. Trout which come by their death in this way have the usually pink parts of a dull white, with the eyes and gills of the same colour, and covered with a thin, white film. This substance is much used in mills on the banks of trout-streams, and probably more fish are destroyed by this kind of pollution in a month than the most inveterate poacher will kill in a year.

Throughout summer fish are in season, but the really serious poaching is practised during close time. Salmon offer fair marks, and the poacher obtains these by spearing. A pronged instrument is driven into the fleshy shoulders of the fish, and it is hauled out on to the bank. In this way sometimes more fish are obtained in a night than can be carried away; and when the gang is chased by watchers the fish have generally to be left behind, as they are difficult things to transport. In one outlying village, during last close season, poached salmon was so common that the cottagers fed their poultry upon it right through the winter. It is said that several fish were taken each over twenty pounds in weight. Another way of securing salmon and trout from the spawning "redds" is by means of "click-hooks." These are simply large salmon-hooks bound together shaft to shaft, and attached to a long cord; a bit of lead balances them, and adds weight. These are used in deep rivers, where spearing by wading is impracticable. When a fish is seen, the hooks are thrown beyond it, and then gently dragged until they come immediately beneath; a sharp "click" usually sends them into the soft

under-parts of the fish, which is then drawn out.
That natural poacher, the pike, is frequently
ridded from trout-streams in this fashion.   Of
course, poaching with click-hooks requires to be
done in the light, or by the aid of an artificial one.
Lights attract salmon and trout just as they
attract birds, and tar-brands are frequently used
by poachers.   Shooting is sometimes resorted to,
but for this class of poaching the habits and
beats of the water-bailiffs require to be accurately
known.   The method has the advantage of being
quick ; and a gun in skilful hands, and at a short
distance, may be used without injuring the fleshy
parts of the body.   That deadly bait, salmon-roe,
is now rarely used, the method of preparing it
having evidently died out with the old-fashioned
poachers, who used it with such effect.

The capture of either poachers or their nets
is often difficult to accomplish.   The former wind
their sinuous way, snake-like, through the wet
meadows in approaching the rivers, and their
nets are rarely kept at home.   These they secrete
about farm buildings, in dry ditches, or among
the bushes in close proximity to their poaching
grounds.   Were they kept at home, the obtaining
of a search-warrant by the police or local angling
association would always render their custody a
critical one.   They are sometimes kept in the

poachers' houses, though only for a short period, when about to be used. At this time the police have found them secreted in the chimney, between a bed and the mattress, or even wound about the portly persons of the poachers' wives. The women are not always simply aiders and abettors, but in poaching sometimes play a more important *rôle*. They have frequently been taken red-handed by the watchers. The vocation of these latter is a hard one. They work at night, and require to be most on the alert during rough and wet weather—in the winter, when the fish are spawning. Sometimes they must remain still for hours in freezing clothes; and in summer they not unfrequently lie all night in dank and wet herbage. They see the night side of nature, and many of them are fairly good naturalists. If a lap-wing gets up and screams in the darkness they know how to interpret the sound, as also a hare rushing wildly past. It must be confessed, however, that at all points the fish-poacher is cleverer and of readier wit than the river-watcher.

XVI

EPHEMERÆ.

OF all nature's beautiful objects submitted to the plyer of the contemplative art, perhaps none are so surpassingly beautiful, or have more exquisite form and colour than the gauzy-winged flies which afford food to the pink-spotted trout. Every one of the angler's months — from dry March to sodden October—brings its own flies, all more or less delectable to the denizens of the streams. We say "more or less" because the fisherman regulates his likes and dislikes by those of the trout, and praises most the fly that the fishes have already passed their verdict upon. Here, for instance, is the black alder. "What shall be said of this queen of flies? O, thou beloved member of the brute creation! Songs have been written in praise of thee; statues would ere now have been erected to thee had that haunchback, and those flabby wings of thine, been 'susceptible of artistic treatment.' But ugly thou art in the eyes of the uninitiated vulgar ; a little, stumpy old maid, toddling about the world in a black bonnet and a brown cloak, laughed at by naughty boys, but doing good wherever thou comest, and leaving sweet memories behind thee ; so sweet that the trout will rise at the ghost or sham of thee, for pure love of thy past kindnesses to them, months after thou hast departed from this sublunary sphere. What hours of bliss do I not owe to thee! How often have I seen in the rich meads of Wey, after picking out wretched quarter-pounders all the morning on March-brown and red-hackle, the great trout rush from every hover to welcome thy first appearance among the sedges and buttercups! How often, late in August, on Thames, on Test, on Lodden heads, have I seen the three and four-pound fish prefer thy dead image to any live reality . . . and the great trout rose and rose, and would not cease, at thee, my alder fly! Have I not seen, after a day when the earth below was iron, and the heavens above as brass, that the three-pounders would have thee, and thee alone, in the purple August dusk, and old Moody's red face grow redder and redder with excitement, half proud at having advised me to 'put on' thee. . . . Beloved alder fly! would that I could give thee a soul (if, indeed, thou hast

not one already, thou and all things which live),
and make thee happy in all *æons* to come! But
as it is, such immortality as I can bestow on thee
here is small return for all the pleasant days thou
hast bestowed on me."

That which Kingsley here expresses for the
black alder is only an echo of what goes forth from
the heart of every angler towards a dozen other
flies which may happen to be his favourite, or the
" killing " fly of his own particular stream. Every
fly-fisher has some speciality with which he has performed doughty deeds, and how anxiously does he
wait for his beloved fly to "come on"! As soon as
the warm weather returns, and the trout begin to
feed, every month brings its more or less season-
able flies. Of these gauzy creatures, which constitute the food of trout, there are myriads ; but of
course the number of species is comparatively
few, and, speaking generally, these are represented
by four great families, representing two general
classes of flies. The *Ephemeræ* are the "up-
winged" flies of anglers ; the *Phryganeæ* the flat-
winged. But with all the myriad water-flies
which constitute the bulk of fish food, there are
a dozen on most streams which carry the angler
right on through the season. Though what "the
season" means in particular districts only the
angler knows. What will kill in one place in

April does not come on elsewhere till June, or in a third locality is over by the middle of March. On the Greenwash, for instance, at the opening of the season the successful flies used are the duns, dressed from light and dark snipe, with sometimes starling and dotterel. The famous "March-browns" float down-stream later than their name would imply, and one of the best of all lures, the May-fly (represented in the north by the stone-fly), does not make its appearance till June, or sometimes July. April and May, if soft and bright, usually present the greatest number of flies, these sometimes seeming to cover the surface of the stream. And here among the grasses and water-avens you might say of a dozen species as has been said of one :

> You find her out on every stalk,
> Whene'er you take a river walk,
> When swifts at eve begin to hawk.

There are duns of every form and colour— gnats and willow-flies, and creepers among the pebbles; and insects, insects everywhere. You can put aside your rod, and lie down among the lush summer grass, and examine them at your leisure. The mechanism of each is wonderful, and all are beautiful. But by carefully observing, you are instantly aroused—as what angler would not be?—

"for is not the green drake on?" asks Kingsley ; "and while he reigns, all hours, meals, decencies, and respectabilities must yield to his caprice. See, here he sits, or rather tens of thousands of him, one on each stalk of grass, green drake, yellow drake, brown drake, white drake, each with his gauzy wings folded on his back, waiting for some unknown change of temperature, or something else, in the afternoon, to wake him from his sleep and send him fluttering over the stream ; while overhead the black drake, who has changed his skin and reproduced his species, dances in the sunshine, empty, hard, and happy."

"For no one will eat him, he well doth know."

XVII

A KING AMONG ANGLERS.

WILSON settled at Elleray immediately upon the close of his brilliant career at Oxford. He seems to have sought out this spot as one in which his whole pure animalism could have full play. And truly he found a fitting environment for a noble mind. Elleray hangs upon one of the slopes of Windermere, and commands a prospect which is perhaps without a parallel in Britain. Immediately below lies the river-lake ; the rich foregrounds are of quiet, exquisite beauty; at the head of the valley the great mountains lock in the landscape ; and finally there is the sense of aërial sublimity which every one has felt who has stood by the cottage. Elleray was literally a cottage when Wilson found it—lichen-covered and overhung by a fine old sycamore. He loved this tree, and in his writings frequently alludes to it : "Never in this well-wooded world, not even in the days of the Druids, could there have been

such another tree! It would be easier to sup-
pose two Shakespeares." Wilson probably found
at Elleray what he sought. He tramped among
the mountains; he, fished; he boated with his
favourite " Billy Balmer " on the lake ; he tended
his game birds and fought mains ; and he certainly
indulged in many boisterous pleasures. The
presence of "the Lakers," as Byron irreverently
dubbed them, might be some inducement to
Wilson, as they certainly had influence as his
neighbours. Wordsworth was at Rydal, Southey
and Coleridge at Keswick, De Quincey with
Wordsworth, and besides these there were other
lesser lights. Strange as it may appear, there
was a good deal in common between these
men, and they were frequently at each other's
houses. Allanbank, the house which Wordsworth occupied after his return from Colerton,
was a common resort ; and whilst here as the
guest of Wordsworth Wilson made the acquaintance of both Coleridge and De Quincey.
At this time all of them were young, and
would seem to have had an intense enjoyment
of life. Excursions among the mountains were
their chief pursuits, and one of these became
memorable. This was an invasion of solitary Eskdale by a little army of anglers, with
tents and baggage for a week's sojourn. It

formed the theme of the "Angler's Tent," one of Wilson's minor poems, a line of which caused considerable discussion among the party. The last of these lines was the awkward one, and it was left as shaped by Wordsworth:

> The placid lake that rested far below,
> Softly embosoming another sky.

A touching incident connected with these mountain rambles was to form the subject of a poem by Wilson; but it was never fulfilled. Wordsworth had a younger brother, who went to sea. Upon one occasion, after a visit home, the poet set out with this brother across the hills, on his way to rejoin his ship. Before parting, the two sat down by Red Tarn, beneath Helvellyn, and talked over future plans of happiness when next they should meet. They also agreed to then and there lay the foundation-stone of a little fishing-hut; and this was done. The brother was subsequently drowned at sea, and Wordsworth afterwards related the incident as stated.

At this time, boating was one of Wilson's great diversions, and he kept quite a fleet of sailing smacks on Windermere. Although the lake is exceedingly treacherous, he and his henchman often started for it at midnight, and had many escapades. Another slight adventure in connection with the lake is worth recounting. Riding one day by

Rydal Water, Wilson's horse became restive, and
to quiet it he turned its head to the lake, intend-
ing to cool its ardour among the oozy reeds.
Soon, however, both man and horse were plunged
beyond their depth, when the latter commenced
to cross. His friend's horse followed the lead,
and both made the passage in safety. Another
midnight escapade may be set down, as it was
one which he dearly loved and frequently indulged.
Soon after De Quincey came to reside in the
Lake District, he describes how he was out at
dawn on a summer morning, when he saw a
cavalcade of six horsemen enveloped in dust come
sweeping down the road. In front was a huge
beast, advancing at a long trot, and experiencing
great difficulty in navigating his unwieldy bulk.
The beast is a bull, and as the flying horsemen
come nearer, each is seen to be armed with a
spear fourteen feet long. The bull gains a rocky
eminence, and stands bellowing and blowing
clouds of smoke from his nostril. Soon, however,
he is dislodged, and, with the hunters at his tail,
goes scouring to the plain below. After a struggle
in the morass of the lake, lasting a quarter of an
hour, and when the bull again seeks higher
ground, Wilson yells: "Turn the villain; turn that
villain, or he will take to Cumberland;" and De
Quincey, having performed the office requested,

soon loses the stampeders round a bend of the road. The bull was not unfrequently turned out at midnight for a fifteen mile burst, and, it is said, became quite used to the nightly visitation.

At Oxford, where was a famous cockpit, Wilson was one of the great "cockers" of his time. At Elleray his game birds engrossed as much time as his boats; and in his walks abroad he usually carried a game-cock under his arm, to pit against those of his neighbours. It is even reported upon trustworthy evidence, that the Professor indulged in the pastime in his drawing-room on Sunday afternoons, and we know that he did so upon one memorable week-day. In his diary are frequent reminders of the sport. Thus: " Black Edinburgh hen set on Tuesday, the 23rd of June, with twelve eggs—middle of the day. Sister to the above was set with five eggs on Thursday, but they had been sat upon a day or two before." And side by side with some beautiful lines from the " Isle of Palms " is ranged " a list of cocks for a main with W. and T.," and then comes " Lord Derby," " Caradice," and the rest of them. Wilson kept only the purest game-fowl, and bred from the best fighting strains in the country. Although this erstwhile moral philosopher was a keen cock-fighter, he was eminently kind and gentle to animals in general. There was not a dumb creature about Elleray but what he had knowledge of and became friends with. He was a keen sportsman, a good naturalist, and of birds he has written some of the best descriptions in the language. It is true that in his outdoor sketches there is but little of the " pretty upholstery of nature," as regards dorsal fins and tail feathers, but each subject he describes is essentially a wild creature in its haunts. " Christopher North," in his sporting jacket, was a familiar figure on the moors, and but few of his friends could tramp through the heather so long or with such success. He was as skilful with the gun as with the rod, and flogging the trout streams in spring was among his chiefest delights. There were none of the old-fashioned country sports in which Wilson did not indulge, and in all he himself was a proficient. If he did not sport his figure in the ring, he attended at all the annual wrestlings, and gave prizes and belts to the competitors. He was not slow to show his strength and prowess in private, and the yeomen and farmers were often treated to an exhibition of his skill. He threw some of the champion wrestlers of the time ; and was also a clever boxer. Anent the repute in which wrestling was held, Wilson tells how a political friend of his, a staunch fellow, in passing through the Lakes, heard of nothing but the contest for the county, and which he understood would lie between Lord Lowther (the sitting member) and Mr. Brougham. But, to his sore perplexity, he heard the names of new candidates, to him hitherto unknown. And on meeting Wilson, he told him with a serious countenance that Lord Lowther would be ousted, for that the struggle, so far as he could learn, would ultimately be between Thomas Ford, of Egremont, and William Richardson, of Caldbeck, men of no landed property, and probably Radicals. This contest was at Carlisle, and had no political complexion whatever.

One of the great resorts of the literary coterie of the Lakes during Wilson's time was the little mountain inn at Wastdale Head, kept by the Tysons. Upon one occasion the Professor proposed a sail on Wastwater, and when well into the middle of the tarn he fell overboard. There was great consternation in the boat, and first one and then another made a grab at him, though to the peril of every one in the tub. Wilson could not restrain his laughter, however, as he was pulled aboard, and the rescuers found that one more prank had been played upon them. Old Tyson describes Wilson as a "fine, gay, girt-hearted fellow, as strang as a lion, an' as lish as a troot, an' he hed sic antics

as nivver man hed." Then he describes a
merry night at Wastdale, and how, upon the
parson coming in, "North" made a song about
him. "He med it reight off o' t' stick end. He
began wi' t' parson first, then he gat t' Pope,
an' then he turned it t' devil. T' parson was
quite astonished, an' rayder vex't an' all, but at
last he burst out laughin' wi' t' rest. He was
like. Naabody could stand it." Wilson was
fond of attending the country balls in the Lake
District, and especially such as were patronised
by a Miss Jane Penny. This lady was "the
anchor," as he expressed it, without whom " he
should keep beating about the great sea of life
to very little purpose."

Wilson's love of angling went with him to
the end. How touching is this picture, drawn
by his daughter, when only a few days remained
to him on earth! Although broken in body,
his spirit went back to the mountain streams
whence he had so often drawn the pink-spotted
trout : " Certain it was the 'mearns' came among
those waking dreams, and then he gathered
around him, when the spring mornings brought
gay jets of sunshine into the little room where
he lay, the relics of a youthful passion, one that
with him never grew old. It was an affecting
sight to see him busy, nay, quite absorbed, with

the fishing-tackle scattered about his bed, propped up with pillows—his noble head, yet glorious with its flowing locks, carefully combed by attentive hands, and falling on each side of his unfaded face. How neatly he picked out each elegantly dressed fly from its little bunch, drawing it out with trembling hand along the white coverlet, and then replacing it in his pocket-book, he would tell ever and anon of the streams he used to fish in of old, and of the deeds he had performed in his childhood and youth. These precious relics of a bygone sport were wont to be brought out in the early spring, long before sickness confined him to his room. It had been a habit of many years, but then the 'sporting jacket' was donned soon after, and angling was no more a mere delightful day-dream, but a reality, 'that took him knee-deep, or waistband-high, through river-feeding torrents, to the glorious music of his running and ringing reel.'"

CHARLES DICKENS AND EVANS, CRYSTAL PALACE PRESS.

SYLVAN FOLK.

By JOHN WATSON.

"A charming book."—*Sheffield Independent.*

"Written by a born naturalist."—*Daily News.*

"Such a book as will astonish and delight unfortunate dwellers in cities."—*Liverpool Daily Post.*

"Whoever admires Jefferies—lover of Nature, or lover of sport—will admire 'Sylvan Folk.'"—*Land and Water.*

"Full of delicate description as enchanting as a fairy tale. Dull, indeed must be the reader who is insensible to its delightful charm."—*Manchester Examiner.*

"It reminds us of Richard Jefferies; and indeed it may be placed on the same shelf with that of the greatest of all writers on English rural life."—*Christian Leader.*

"Richard Jefferies' mantle has fallen on John Watson's shoulders. May he long be spared to give us other books as true to nature and as charmingly written as 'Sylvan Folk.'"—*Guardian.*

"It is this freshness, this outdoor atmosphere, that leads the reader along in fascinated interest from the first to the last page."—*Literary World.*

"Pages of authority for all who angle or who shoot, who find their delight in the wood, their ecstasy on the moor, or their heaven upon earth at the waterside."—*Rod and Gun.*

"His descriptions are so fresh—they suggest so vividly the idea of happy hours spent among attractive scenes in the open air—that they will give genuine pleasure to every one who reads them."—*Nature.*

"A sympathetic, keen-eyed, worshipful observer of Nature, Mr. Watson writes with the simplicity and directness of a man who knows what he is about. There is not an uninteresting page in 'Sylvan Folk' from first to last."—*Echo.*

"As we had occasion to speak favourably of Mr. Watson's 'A Year in the Fields,' it gives us much pleasure to say that his new book is in every sense worthy of it, and of the reputation which it brought its author."—*Spectator.*

www.ingramcontent.com/pod-product-compliance
Lightning Source LLC
Chambersburg PA
CBHW030555270326
41927CB00007B/937